HEINEMANN SCHOOL MANAGEMENT

Managing the Arts in the Curriculum

by
Michael Marland and Rick Rogers

Heinemann Educational Publishers
Halley Court, Jordan Hill, Oxford OX2 8EJ
a division of Reed Educational and Professional Publishing Ltd

OXFORD   MELBOURNE   AUCKLAND
JOHANNESBURG   BLANTYRE   GABORONE
IBADAN   PORTSMOUTH (NH)   USA   CHICAGO

Heinemann is a registered trademark of Reed Educational and Professional Publishing Ltd

Text © Michael Marland and Rick Rogers, 2002

First published in 2002

06 05 04 03 02
10 9 8 7 6 5 4 3 2 1

All rights reserved.

Apart from any fair dealing for the purposes of research or private study, or criticism or review as permitted under the terms of the UK Copyright, Designs and Patents Act, 1988, this publication may not be reproduced, stored or transmitted, in any form or by any means, without the prior permission in writing of the publishers, or in the case of reprographic reproduction only in accordance with the terms of the licences issued by the Copyright Licensing Agency in the UK, or in accordance with the terms of the licences issued by the appropriate Reproduction Rights Organization outside the UK. Enquiries concerning reproduction outside the terms stated here should be sent to the publishers at the address printed on this page.

British Library Cataloguing in Publication Data
A catalogue record for this book is available from the British Library

ISBN 0 435 80056 6

Typeset by J&L Composition Ltd, Filey, North Yorkshire
Printed and bound in Great Britain by Biddles Ltd, Guildford

The publishers have made every effort to contact copyright holders. However, if any material has been incorrectly acknowledged, the publishers would be pleased to correct this at the earliest opportunity.

Websites
Links to appropriate websites are given throughout the book. Although these were up to date at the time of writing, it is essential for teachers to preview these sites before using them with students. This will ensure that the web address (URL) is still accurate and the content is suitable for your needs. We suggest that you bookmark useful sites and consider enabling students to access them through the school intranet.

We are bringing this to your attention as we are aware of legitimate sites being appropriated illegally by people wanting to distribute unsuitable or offensive materials. We strongly advise you to purchase suitable screening software so that students are protected from unsuitable sites and their material. If you do find that the links given no longer work, or the content is unsuitable, please let us know. Details of changes will be posted on our website.

Tel: 01865 888058 www.heinemann.co.uk

Contents

	INTRODUCTION	1
1	**THE PLACE OF THE ARTS IN SCHOOL EDUCATION**	**5**
	1.1 The overall arts curriculum philosophy	5
	1.2 Contribution to the education of the whole person	9
	1.3 Legal requirements	12
	1.4 Partners in the arts curriculum	15
2	**THE RANGE OF THE ARTS**	**19**
	2.1 Planning breadth and depth	19
	2.2 The intercultural aspects	20
	2.3 The art forms	25
3	**PLANNING ACROSS THE SCHOOL**	**61**
	3.1 Auditing the school's arts provision	61
	3.2 Pupils as creators, performers and audience	73
	3.3 Whole-school curriculum planning for the arts	77
	3.4 Aspects of the arts in other courses and tutorial sessions	85
	3.5 Other curriculum content in arts courses	94
4	**DELIVERY**	**118**
	4.1 The communal life of the school	118
	4.2 The use of public arts	127
	4.3 Devising the specific arts courses	132
	4.4 Presenting the artwork of pupils	134
5	**SUPPORTING THE DELIVERY**	**139**
	5.1 Funding and resourcing	139
	5.2 Accommodation and facilities	148
	5.3 Technicians and support staff	153
	5.4 Partnerships and evaluation	156
	Appendix 1 Arts and Curriculum Organisations	164
	Appendix 2 Trusts and Foundations for Arts Funding Support	165
	References	166
	Index	170

Acknowledgements

We are very grateful indeed for what we have learned from the very many artists, teachers, pupils, parents, workers in national and local organisations and members of working parties and committees whom we have collaborated with, observed, in whose organisations we have worked, or on whose committees we have sat. Also, we would like to express our gratitude to the authors of the range of writing and the research studies that we have read and from which we have learned. Whilst we of course accept full responsibility for any errors of fact or judgement in the book, we would like to stress how much we have valued the contribution of all those people to the place of arts in our schools.

For permission to use material on carrying out an arts audit, originally commissioned by the Society, we are grateful to the Royal Society for the encouragement of Arts, Manufactures and Commerce (RSA). We are similarly grateful to the Calouste Gulbenkian Foundation, the Arts Council of England, and Professor Malcolm Ross for permission to quote from their reports.

Among the many individuals who contributed suggestions and ideas or checked facts for us, we would like to thank specifically: Murray Aikman, Liz Bowden, David Coleman of Sport England, David Gee, David Hargreaves, Keith Critchlow, Kalyan Kundu, Fran Little, Shivanti Lowton, Linda Marsh, Beryl McAlhone, Rachel Moses, Mark Pattenden, Phillipa Reive, Maggie Semple, Charlotte Stone, Sheila Stone, Michael Turner, and Jack Whitehead.

We would like to thank Jane Moses for her skilled word-processing and coordination of the text.

Michael Marland and Rick Rogers

Introduction

It is wise for both secondary and primary schools, in the spirit and within the letter of the national requirements, to have an overview of the arts in the whole-school curriculum and all its modes of delivery, rather than merely adding one arts course and another together. School curriculum planning should be, and was designed by the underlying 1988 legislation to be, over-arching – incorporating the requirements of the National Curriculum, but not shaped or controlled by them.

Before the place of the arts in the whole-school curriculum can be planned, a school needs what is in effect both a philosophical and logistical review of the questions of 'What are the arts?' and 'Why are they to be in our curriculum?' It then needs to link those to: 'What are the central government requirements?'

After the first decade of the National Curriculum imposition, there has been a national revival of encouragement for the arts, especially in the report of the National Advisory Committee on Creative and Cultural Education: *All Our Futures: Creativity, Culture and Education* (1999). Since about then, there has been an increasing government emphasis on 'creativity' across the curriculum up through the years.

There is no central blueprint – each school has to define its own philosophy, using government guidelines, but also to develop it. This book is designed to enable schools to further review and plan their overall arts policy in relation to the whole-school curriculum and pastoral policy.

The arts are strongly personal and individual. This makes it difficult to plan the place they should occupy in an organised curriculum. The arts celebrate. They offer a moment of perfection in an imperfect world. They move and they deepen emotion. They often help in the understanding of life and they offer, in the words of I. A. Richards, 'a storehouse of recorded values' (Richards, 1932). Above all, they delight. In the exigencies and pressures of the school day, it can be very difficult to organise opportunities for delight, and the trouble with things that offer delight is that they are not going to delight everybody all of the time. This gives us one of our hardest curriculum-planning and pedagogical challenges.

Further, studies of what aspect of the arts come to excite individuals, and how and when, reveal that there is often a kind of serendipity associated with them. It is frequently a piece of music, a painting, or a book, come across by chance, that proves to have the greatest significance. There are, of course, deliberate acts and rational choices, but extension and growth often result from unexpected juxtapositions and the generous enthusiasm of others.

In his research paper 'The Teaching of Art and the Art of Teaching', David Hargreaves records six aims that visual arts teachers gave for their work: personal and emotional development, visual awareness, skill training, compensation, education for leisure, and initiation in our cultural heritage (Hargreaves, 1983, pp.130–1). Other teachers could doubtless have added to the list. Some people tend to overplay one simple aim, or to choose some of the more obscure and unlikely aims (for example, 'help develop a self-image') and neglect the breadth and variety. We have to explore a more varied, more flexible, and not too dogmatic or exclusive set of justifications. When an adult amateur pianist plays (at a very simple level) one of Mendelssohn's *Songs Without Words*, he does not think 'I'm improving my self-image'; or that he or she is finding 'a realised form' (Witkin, 1974, pp.46–9).

It may be going too far to say, as some supporters of the arts in education would, that arts in schools 'educate children's emotions', but they give a great deal to the children's already growing emotions and help the pupils to develop their emotional range and depth further. Essentially, we are not planning for the arts, but planning for people – and that is a difficult curriculum aim.

Some years ago, the then Inner London Education Authority leader, Frances Morrell, declared:

> It is not simply a matter of unlocking the doors of human artistic achievement to pupils and students. The arts are central to the curriculum because they liberate the forces of creative thinking and doing which are as vital to the educational process as the other key disciplines.

(Morrell, 1983)

The Qualifications and Curriculum Authority's (QCA) predecessor, the School's Council, reported in 1975: 'Arts education remains a matter of only peripheral concern. Neither the arts subjects nor the teachers have ever been taken seriously' (Ross, 1975). We can look, for instance, at what has happened to Dance. Despite marvellous work by skilled enthusiasts, often in their own time, Dance seemed to be in the weakest position of all the arts in school at that time. The Gulbenkian Report in 1980 on Dance education spoke of the 'generally meagre and confused place occupied by Dance in the British Secondary'. 'Dance is taught in only one third of our sample ... rarely taught beyond the first three years, and is restricted almost entirely to girls' (Calouste Gulbenkian, 1980, pp.54, 55). How much better are those figures in the twenty-first century?

The so-called *Framework for the Curriculum* mentioned that children have to appreciate human achievements and aspirations, but hardly mentioned the arts at all. There appeared to be an aesthetic vacuum in central Government thinking. It is not surprising that the National Association for Education in the Arts spoke so bitterly about the DES 5–16 curriculum outline (DES, 1984), declaring it to be 'a clunk-click curriculum, secure and strapped down, the answer to an administrator's prayer but, alas, sadly impoverished as a structure to support human learning or as an induction into life'.

In the teaching profession we stereotype the arts as impracticable, while science is regarded as totally logical. Yet the biologist Peter Medawar points out in 'Intuition and Induction in Science' that there is far less induction and far more intuition than scientists pretend (Medawar, 1977). Overall, we think there is a lack of interest in the arts in the teaching profession as a whole and the interest that does exist is under-used by the specialist arts teachers. We are all somewhat modest in schools; amateur musicians and artists often keep quiet. It can be years before the relevant department finds out that a colleague likes playing the piano or another sings in a choir.

A series of government reports over the years have spoken approvingly of the place of our subject in schools, but the schools have hardly responded. How many of the ideas in Haddow (Consultative Committee of the Board of Education, 1926), Crowther, Newsom and Plowden (Central Advisory Council for Education, 1959, 1963 and 1967) have been taken up? When the Newsom report *Half our Future*, came out, many thought that there was about to be a strong new expansion, but its thrust was not followed until revived in 2000. Its 'extended day' for the arts similarly went ignored for many years.

The Plowden Report (1967) confirmed the need for a child-centred and coherent curriculum approach, stressing that:

> Art is both a form of communication and a means of expression of feelings which ought to permeate the whole curriculum and the whole life of the school.... It affects, or should affect, all aspects of our life from the design of the common-place articles of everyday life to the highest forms of individual expression.
>
> (Central Advisory Council, 1967, p.267)

However, it has been extremely difficult to have a strong coverage of all the arts with sufficient specialism. The proper planning of education in the arts in a school requires a whole-school curriculum policy on the arts, which would illuminate all the subjects, the pastoral programme, and the wider life of the school. It should work from broad aims to detailed targets, even specifying numerical targets for visits by pupils, and certainly describing the range of experiences hoped for.

Schools should create a community in which the arts matter and in which parents and teachers are convinced of this. Despite the problems which teachers face, there are more immense potentialities in this century for all the arts in school than there have been previously. It should be possible through more thorough, inventive, sensitive, coherent, and intense planning in schools, to realise those potentialities.

In May 2000, QCA published guidance on the foundation stages curriculum which included advice on how to promote children's creative development. The key principal officer, Tony Knight, declared: 'The arts are a powerful means of exploring and communicating our common and different cultures'. We have to strengthen our vision of the arts as contributing to all aspects of human growth, enriching life and illuminating it, and the arts should be culturally wide in period and cultural tradition, in genre, form, and also across many aspects of the curriculum.

Our book has been written after a wide review of recent movements in thinking about the arts curriculum. These are viewed in the light of legislative requirements and more general central direction, as well as the practicalities of school management, staffing, facilities, and curriculum planning. We address the aims and possibilities of the arts in all schools – and in some ways the challenges facing secondary and primary are very similar (for example, cultural breadth and inter-curricular relationships), though most of our examples are drawn from secondary schools. For both, the arts suffered in the last decade of the last century, but the present vision and hopes for expansion are very encouraging.

1 THE PLACE OF ARTS IN SCHOOL EDUCATION

1.1 The overall arts curriculum philosophy

In Europe up until the early nineteenth century, great works of art were nearly all in palaces, churches, or the homes of the wealthy collectors. A new idea then grew that everyone should be able to enjoy great paintings and that this was good for society as a whole. The founding of the National Gallery with just 38 paintings in 1824 marked the start of that movement in Britain. Now, the National Gallery has over 2000 paintings and four million people visit it every year. That broadening movement came to widespread fruition years ago and the secondary curriculum should reflect that.

Nevertheless, we are often reticent about bringing the full range of major art before the young. Perhaps in our knowledge-based and somewhat scholarly age, there is too much fear of 'the great' and an inappropriate respect, leading to doubts about ordinary human reactions. Yet we should start with the very young and allow them to show ordinary human interest. The author of an art book for young children put it simply and accurately:

> Introducing children to art is as easy as opening a book, and the rewards are enormous. For thousands of years people have expressed themselves through art, so there is much to see and a great deal to learn. By giving children just a few pictures, you can open up this world of infinite richness and diversity for them to explore. As you look at these pictures with a child, talk about anything that springs to mind – the expression on a face, the pattern on a dress, or even the colour of the sky. Talk about how a picture makes you both feel. Is it a happy picture or a sad one? Is it noisy or quiet? Imagine that you can climb right into the pictures together – rolling hoops in a playground scene or defending a castle under siege.

(Micklethwait, 1996, p.8)

From a very early age, children should be taught to look and to really *see*. This needs broadening, deepening, and sharpening in the secondary school. This art and skill should be taught for all aspects of the physical environment – the streetscape, buildings, artefacts, people, newspapers, television and film, sculpture, and pictures.

The arts contribute to the education of the eye, the ear, the mind, the emotions, and the body. They should not be seen merely as separate courses, for they illuminate the study of language, technology, and most aspects of humanity, including culture and social development. The arts both enrich life and illuminate it. They lie at the centre of most cultures, yet despite dedicated arts teachers they lie fragmented around the periphery of many schools in the UK and some other countries – and many of these teachers feel their professional life is fragmented also.

Often we have not defined what the arts are for, or even what they are, in schools. We find it most difficult because some of the values are not amenable to educational analysis. It is very difficult in the didactic structure of school to share things you care about, particularly as sometimes you do not have an intellectual reason for that caring. Love has little place in the curriculum and its inclusion cannot easily be justified, yet it lies at the centre of the arts. How then can schools plan so that pupils will have true access to arts, which move emotion, help an understanding of life, offer a series of recorded values, but, above all, offer that hardest thing to schedule – delight!

In the UK since 1988, 'cultural development' has been a national legal requirement for every school's curriculum. However, we have had a very strange and patchy legacy and there are still lingering worries about provision. At the end of World War II, the central leadership saw only a very limited place for the arts. 'Ministry of Education Pamphlet No. 1' saw some place for the arts and crafts in the secondary modern school to help occupy the minds of pupils of lower intellect and attainment. It was intended primarily to prevent adult boredom in future jobs requiring no skill or interest. Here is the 1945 government dream for the future of most people:

> It has to be remembered that in these schools will be a considerable number of children whose future employment will not demand any measure of technical skill or knowledge. As the mechanisation of industry increases . . . there will be a growing field of routine and repetitive process work. This will present a definite educational problem. There are large numbers of persons who find in their work the mental stimulus and the creative satisfaction that they need, but there are, and will be, much larger numbers whose work may in itself offer little, if anything, to keep minds alert and interests alive. For these their education must

provide the resources, and must develop within themselves the resources, to find and pursue interests which will add to the meaning and enjoyment of life . . . It is partly for this reason that a wide range of crafts and other activities have been practised in the best senior schools and will be developed further in the secondary (modern) schools. They stimulate initiative, exactness and a variety of interests. Some of which may well lay the foundation of future leisure-time occupations.

(Ministry of Education, 1945, p.20)

Thus, the UK came out of the war with a very limited arts ambition for schools, a trace of which still lingers. For instance, in a very popular book written by an LEA's Director of Education for national publication three years after the war, *Old Bottles and New Wine*, there was only a hint that the arts should be specifically taught:

All, it is true, must receive training in aesthetic and moral values, but this should grow incidentally out of lessons of all kinds. It may be held that English as a subject gives sufficient scope in itself for aesthetic training. But it is also a tenable idea that some time should be devoted to specific instruction in the appreciation of art and music. If this is accepted it must, albeit reluctantly, be accepted that the time that can be afforded for such appreciative work is small.

(Mander, 1948, p.38)

At least he included the specific teaching of 'Art and Music (Appreciation)', though significantly only as 'a tenable idea'.

Even in many strong comprehensive schools with skilled teachers, art was for many years 'ghettoised' in 'The Art Department'. A major, published description of Creighton School, a comprehensive school in the mid-seventies, stressed the isolation of the visual arts.

In the school as a whole, in the main public entrance halls and thoroughfares, there is no sign that they have an Art department. There had been a display on a corner of the main hall in the North Wing when I'd first arrived at the school in September, but that had soon gone. . . . The interior of the school as a whole is visually depressing, with long, undecorated concrete corridors and blank walls, blank save for scuff marks low down from thousands of passing feet and the occasional graffiti higher up, away from the arms of the cleaners. Girls' schools usually make an attempt to make their surroundings attractive, whether private or state. Primary schools are always a blaze of colour, texture, visual activity and excitement. But mixed comprehensives, especially the larger ones, so often seem oblivious to their surroundings. Judging by the corridor walls at Creighton, you might be forgiven for thinking that the pupils never produce any visual work, in Art or in any other lessons.

(Davies, 1976, p.115)

Over the years there were many strong efforts, but still major difficulties remained. Just over twenty years ago a national UK survey reported:

> Arts education remains a matter of only peripheral concern; neither the arts subject or the arts teachers have ever been taken seriously. Such has been the conclusion of every major education report published in the last fifteen years and such is ours.
>
> (Ross, 1975)

Arts educators have often felt that they were fighting against denigrating pressures. In 1978, looking ahead to the new millennium, the then Arts Curriculum Project had a conference on 'Arts Education: Towards 2000'. Its director, Malcolm Ross said: 'The Education Debate and the Green Paper seem to herald a more virulent materialism, a more mechanistic ethic' (Ross, 1978). Many would argue strongly that the nineties carried those limitations even further and the definition of the National Curriculum in the 1988 and 1996 legislation and its interpretation lowered the scope and status of the arts in schools. Further, the National Literacy Strategy and Numeracy Strategy at the end of the decade, whilst not strictly part of the National Curriculum, were treated as mandatory and further reduced the place of the arts in the primary school. Indeed, some consider that the artistic aspects of literature have been cramped by the approach to 'literacy' in the Strategy.

Thus, in planning for the future of the arts in the secondary school it is realistic to analyse the difficulties. In the UK at least we do not have as strong a tradition as some say we do and we have inherited many difficulties:

- a lack of trust of the power of arts;
- doubts of the impact on children;
- fears of the lack of support by parents;
- limited arts training for many teachers;
- the denigration by some specialist teachers of the core skills;
- very little dance across the country, with few boys involved and limited time;
- poor working conditions and sometimes very limited specialist facilities;
- limited use of visiting artists;
- too much emphasis on 'workshops' and not enough on performance.

'Creativity' is an important concept that obviously has a major part in all arts courses. There have been times, though, when some schools have seen this human skill as being at odds with learning about and appreciating the range of the arts. In fact these two aspects interact and are complementary: inventing requires knowledge. Sir Joshua Reynolds put it powerfully in a statement in the late eighteenth century that should illuminate every school's arts curriculum:

> *Invention, strictly speaking, is little more than a new combination of those images which have been previously gathered and deposited in the memory. Nothing can be made of nothing; he who has laid up no materials can produce no combinations.*

Every school should have a clear vision of the key place of the arts. The curriculum plan for a school should incorporate the arts for personal growth, the development of morality (for example, not teaching a moral precept but the humanity under-pinning morality), information-handling skills, the observation and understanding of the environment, culture, history, and occupations. In the UK the National Association for Education in the Arts gave a good over-arching view in 1989:

> *Any valid arts programme in schools must seek to equip pupils with the ability to appreciate the arts both as receivers and practitioners and not only whilst they are at school but throughout their lives. The experience of art should be a disciplined and structured process that develops pupils' skills, and their capacity to think and to solve problems, so as to enable the engagement of the whole personality in acts of understanding.*

1.2 Contribution to the education of the whole person

One way of analysing the school's overall curriculum is to see a major aspect as 'the pastoral curriculum'. This includes those parts which specifically support the school's task of enabling the pupil to develop as a person, usually termed 'Personal, Social and Health Education' (PSHE). Primary schools usually have a clear definition of the curriculum function of enabling self-development, and all secondary schools have a 'pastoral' structure and some pattern of tutoring. There is what the Americans call 'the home-room program', which in the UK is called the tutorial session. More recently, the UK has named as a 'subject' a key aspect of the whole curriculum, 'Citizenship', which is linked in the National Curriculum description with PSHE (c.f. pp.109 –112).

In planning the whole-school arts curriculum, the 'four inter-related sections' of 'the knowledge, skills, and understanding to be taught' should be looked at with the possible arts contribution in mind:

1. Developing confidence and responsibility and making the most of their abilities;
2. Preparing to play an active role as citizens;
3. Developing a healthy, safer lifestyle;
4. Developing good relationships and respecting the differences between people.

(QCA, 2000, p.4)

Certainly the arts can contribute to 1, 2, and 4. The fuller statement of Citizenship lists many personal aspects, as shown on page 109.

Many of these points require both 'specific' and 'contextual' teaching. The arts can contribute to aspects of 'spiritual development, moral development, social development, and cultural development'.

The pastoral aspect of a secondary curriculum focuses on: 'Who am I?' This is what the psychologist Erik Erikson so astutely called 'the central adolescent task' of facing 'the crisis of identity'. It requires an answer to the question: 'What do I want to make of myself and what do I have to work with?' (Erikson, 1971, p.314) The arts are key facets of the whole, for they are a way of exploring self and society, and need systematising for the student to understand their use in personal life.

The range of what the arts contribute to a person's personal education were well described in the 1982 Gulbenkian report *The Arts in Schools: principles, practice and provision* as six areas of educational responsibility:

a developing the full variety of human intelligence;

b developing the capacity for creative thought and action;

c the education of feeling and sensibility;

d developing physical and perceptual skills;

e the exploration of values;

f understanding the changing social culture.

(Calouste Gulbenkian Foundation, 1982, p. 141)

The NFER three-year study *Arts Education in Secondary Schools: Effects and effectiveness* (October 2000) identifies seven direct learning outcomes for pupils attributable to the arts:

- heightened sense of enjoyment, excitement, fulfilment and therapeutic release of tensions;
- increase in knowledge and skills associated with particular art forms;
- enhanced knowledge of social and cultural issues;
- development of creativity and thinking skills;
- enrichment of communication and expressive skills;
- advances in personal and social development;
- effects that transfer to other contexts, such as learning in other subjects, the world of work and cultural activities outside of and beyond school.

The specific teaching of PSHE and Citizenship, tutoring and pastoral care, and the whole-school ethos are essential to the growing child's development. Yet it is important also to appreciate the deep, sensitive, practical, and emotional importance of the arts as a powerful contribution to the personal and social education of the pupil as a person. (See Chapter 3, Section 5 for detailed suggestions.)

The Calouste Gulbenkian Foundation's 'framework for personal and social development' *Passport* points out, for instance, that one of the 'key opportunities . . . which pupils might expect during their school career' is 'to perform for an audience, individually or as part of a group' (Lees and Plant, 2000, p.21). Further, its list of the 'knowledge' required to 'develop good relationships and respect the difference between people' includes much of the human content of many arts course, for instance:

1. Know what we do that makes each other happy, sad and cross, and what helps and what hinders friendships.
2. Know that people live their lives in different ways and that different cultures may have different life patterns.
3. Know that people's response to ideas and events may be determined by age, religion, culture.
4. Develop understanding of different types of relationship including marriage, and know that there are many different patterns of friendship.
5. Understand what families are and what members expect of each other.
6. Know how to deal with friendship problems.

7. Understand more about the changes that take place in human life – parenthood, bereavement, making new relationships.

8. Know about bullying, why it happens, its effects on people, how to deal with it and how to stop it happening.

9. Understand how media messages affect attitudes and can cause inequality of opportunity.

10. Know that human sexuality is expressed in different ways, understand what it means and have some words to describe it.

(Calouste Gulbenkian Foundation, 1982, p.27)

In many ways, the core of the contribution of the arts to the overall curriculum is the emphasis on values. The personal and social development of the pupil gains from a full approach to the arts with a specific focus on the broadening and deepening that the pupil experiences as creator, performer, and audience. A distinguished critic, I. A. Richards, put this clearly in the early twentieth century:

> *The Arts are our storehouse of recorded values. . . . They record the most important judgements we possess as to the values of experience. They form a body of evidence which . . . has been left almost untouched by professed students of value. An odd omission, for without the existence of the Arts we can compare very few of our experiences, and without such comparison we could hardly hope to agree as to which are to be preferred.*

(Richards, 1924, p.32)

1.3 Legal Requirements

Everyone working in or with schools has to do so within the national statutory requirements, and in the last twelve years of the last century there were more extensive changes in those statutory regulations with more detailed requirements than ever before. The very positive *Education Act 1944* had the clearly stated aim of increasing central government power. The Deputy Secretary of the then Board of Education described it as 'an admirable opportunity for re-establishing the position of the Board as the body competent to lead and to direct the educational system of the country'. Despite the strong intention to 'lead rather than follow' the LEAs, for forty-plus years after that Act it was often not clear where power lay, to whom criticisms and suggestions should be made, or who decided what. This vagueness made educational leadership and review and planning difficult. The advantages of that structural vagueness were flexibility and freedom to develop; the disadvantages were confusion and some yawning gaps.

The Labour Government's establishment of a Select Committee in 1978, chaired by Christopher Price, led to the *Education Reform Act 1988*, which introduced the concept of the 'National Curriculum'. From the point of view of the arts there was a significant addition to the overarching requirement of 'the curriculum for the school', which is logically prior and hierarchically superior to the later 'National Curriculum' section:

> *The curriculum for a maintained school satisfies the requirements of this section if it is a balanced and broadly based curriculum which*
>
> *(a) promotes the spiritual, moral, cultural, mental and physical development of the pupils at the school and of society; and*
> *(b) prepares such pupils for the opportunities, responsibilities and experiences of adult life.*
>
> (*Education Reform Act, 1988*, Section 1)

The words in (a) were a repeat of the 1944 wording with one very significant addition: 'culture'. Since then the general arts provision for the pupils has been stronger overall. However, the heavier 'subject' requirements, for instance in Key Stage 4 until 'disapplication' was allowed in 1999, have also limited the arts range of some schools.

The very phrase 'National Curriculum' has led to a deep misunderstanding which was exacerbated by the introductory wording of the government's booklets for schools because they over-used that term and under-used 'the school curriculum'. More recently, the DfEE and the Qualifications and Curriculum Authority have stated in the opening section of both the primary and secondary editions of the *Handbook*:

> *The school curriculum comprises all learning and other experiences that each school plans for its pupils. The National Curriculum is an important element of the school curriculum.*
>
> (DfEE and QCA, 1999, p.10)

Perhaps what is needed is the use of upper case for both titles, not only for the 'national' one! The important point is that the National Curriculum requirements should be regarded as the bottom-line criteria of content, not the overall plan. The 'School Curriculum' has to be planned by the individual school, whilst ensuring that the 'National Curriculum' content is included – in whatever form the school considers best.

One of the major troubles that we have had and the team working on the *Education Reform Act* had to face is the vagueness and confusion about analytic concepts for the curriculum as a whole and the lack of agreement about terminology. Two technical terms in the legislation caused confusion and it is worth clarifying:

(a) *'Subjects':* In schools and colleges this term is used for the sessions to which one goes, usually with the same teacher, for a planned sequence of study. The school timetable is made up of what are usually called 'subjects'. However, in educational philosophy 'subject' is a division of knowledge. There was no intention behind the legislation that the content of the 'core and foundation subjects' as specified in the statutory orders should be co-terminous with the division of the school day decided by the school. Indeed, whilst the act was a bill before Parliament the civil servant in charge realised from many people's comments that the education profession had come to consider that the legislation was determining how to divide up knowledge into the sequences of teaching. In the Act in 1988 wording was specially put in to remove this confusion, and this was re-stated in the *Education Act 1996*:

> An order made under subsection (2) may not require –
>
> (a) the allocation of any particular period or periods of time during any key stage to the teaching of any programme of study or any matter, skill or process forming part of it, or
>
> (b) the making in school timetables of provision of any particular kind for the periods to be allocated to such teaching during any such stage.
>
> (Section 356)

('Subsection 2' is the one specifying the 'subjects' of the National Curriculum.)

Thus we recommend that schools use the term 'course' for the timetabled teaching lessons, retaining 'subject' as the divisions of the planning of the overall curriculum.

(b) *'Programmes of study':* The 1988 legislation required the Secretary of State to 'specify in relation to each of the foundation subjects . . . (b) such programmes of study . . . as he considers appropriate for that subject'. Thus the early National Curriculum official documents used the term 'programmes of study', which led readers to see the list more like a 'syllabus' than a 'contents check list'. Indeed, the term 'programme' means the 'sequence and content'. The more recent Qualifications and Curriculum Authority specifications instead use the phrase: 'Teaching requirements for each subject', which is somewhat clearer that these are not 'programme' sequences.

We must avoid the tendency, then, to think that the 'subjects' listed in the National Curriculum have to be taught in courses so labelled and as divided. Even Ofsted sometimes slip into this error of phrasing. For instance in *The Arts Inspected* the text states:

The National Curriculum requires that all maintained schools teach dance (as part of physical education) in Key Stages 1 and 2, art and music in Key Stages 1 to 3, and drama (as part of English) in Key Stages 1 to 4.

(Ofsted, 1998, p.3)

The phrases in brackets are misleading. The *Handbooks* describe the content under those headings, but there is no requirement that they have to be taught as part of those 'courses'. As the *Handbooks* state: 'It is for schools to choose how they organise their school curriculum to include the programmes of study.' (DfEE and QCA, 1999, primary p.17 and secondary p.18) Dance is not compulsory in Key Stage 3. Schools have to include 'games activities' and choose three out of five activities 'at least one of which must be dance or gymnastic activities' (ibid., secondary, p.177). Although not mentioned by Ofsted in *The Arts Inspected*, aspects of 'the media' and 'moving images' are clearly included in the 'English' course content, though, like 'drama', the location of the teaching in a course is to be decided by the school.

It is commonly assumed that if the National Curriculum requires a 'subject' in a particular Key Stage or Stages it is legally required throughout that time. This is not the wording of the statutory orders, and the Handbook clearly confirms that there is flexibility within a key stage. 'Schools have some discretion over when to start teaching the key stage programmes of study, as the law requires that programmes of study should be taught during the key stage, not that they be introduced at a particular time' (QCA, 1999, p.16). (We have covered the statutory regulations relating to the 'collective act of worship' under 'assemblies' on p.120.)

Finally, the 'teaching requirements' in the *Handbook* in their revised version for the 2000 changes are carefully, sensitively, thoughtfully, and accurately worded. There is almost nothing that an imaginative arts-focussed school would wish to include that could be ruled out by the requirements, and the listed aspects that have to be included are a good basis for in-school planning.

1.4 Partners in the arts curriculum

More than any other curriculum area, the arts have the potential to influence and benefit almost every aspect of school life, and to embrace every group involved in the school. Everyone has a stake in their school running effective, inclusive, and wide-ranging arts provision – pupils, staff, parents, governors, local communities, and the artists and arts organisations near the school. The arts can help to bind together the vital partnerships on which a school relies for its success as an inclusive and vibrant learning centre for a community. The range of the arts' contribution to education can be described as thus:

> Education develops and encourages individual skills, knowledge and understanding in, through and about the arts by participation, observation and appreciation. Education through the arts can be an end in itself as well as being an important contributor to the emotional and spiritual development of the individual and society as a whole.
>
> (ACE, 1996)

Crucially, the world at large acknowledges it too. A MORI poll on public attitudes to the arts (ACE and MORI, August 2000) found that:

- 95% of the general public believe that all schoolchildren should have the opportunity to learn a musical instrument or poetry, or to take part in plays and other arts activities; and
- 82% of the general public believe that the arts help children to achieve more in school.

These attitudes can help a school build a wide range of support and partnerships. They are required because the goals outlined here need more resources and expertise than schools can themselves provide. There are two types of partners. Those with direct involvement in or commitment to the school (staff and governors, pupils and their parents or carers) and those beyond the school where collaboration can bring mutual benefits (local community groups and individuals, local artists arts organisations and other schools).

There are two reasons why a school should identify and build partnerships with these people. First, mutual benefits can flow from such collaborations; second, such wide-ranging involvement can increase the effectiveness of the school's arts provision. For example, a school can benefit from the artistic skills and enthusiasms of parents, governors and others. In turn, these groups can use the facilities offered by the school to enhance those same skills and enthusiasms.

Parents can be a valuable support for their children by encouraging them to be involved in the arts from early childhood and by cultivating an arts-oriented family environment. This can help their child to get more out of a school's arts provision, thereby making it more effective.

The arts can help to develop a school ethos based on, and promoting, creativity across the curriculum. The emphasis is on learning and understanding, access and taking part. It assumes a creative, challenging and qualitative collaboration between schools and artists and their work – irrespective of age, gender, culture, financial or social status, physical or mental ability, or educational achievement.

Key questions

Such an overarching approach to the arts means that a school can develop partnerships that offer mutual benefits, improve the effectiveness of its provision for the arts, and enhance the outcomes of having an effective arts programme.

A school might ask itself what is the purpose of the arts in the context of the school as a whole and in what ways can each person in the school contribute to that purpose? The answers must match the school's ability, current and potential, to deliver its artistic ambitions or creative vision. This means translating those ambitions into planning strategies and objectives, backed by sufficient human, financial and physical resources and integrating the arts into the school's activities and structure.

Several questions are worth asking at this point:

- Does everyone in the school understand what is meant by arts education and its potential across the curriculum?
- Does the school have a single, unifying vision for the arts?
- If not, how might it build and establish such a unifying vision?
- How far, and in what ways, may the arts be further integrated into the school's life and ethos?

Key tasks

The first step is to agree a definition of and vision for the arts which fits the school as a whole. This enables people involved in each curriculum and organisational area to:

- understand the aims, work, and responsibilities of the arts staff; and
- discover how they might relate to help to sustain that work.

In turn, it can enable the arts staff to relate more effectively with the other aspects of the school.

This leads on to a second, parallel, step: defining what greater arts integration might mean for the school. There are some basic parameters within which an 'integrated' school has to work (see below). But each school can develop an approach to integration which best meets its collective needs – artistic, curricular, developmental, and organisational.

This means that an organisation is itself learning in order to provide learning opportunities for all partners. For example, the school might look at how to:

- extend understanding and enjoyment of each other's work;
- help others to develop and experiment with ideas and practical skills through group and individual work; and
- build the additional skills, experience and resources within the school to promote its artistic, educational and administrative development.

Where to start

Every school needs a firm base from which to explore these key questions and tackle these key tasks. Having such a foundation can create a confidence in those who design, organise and deliver such provision. It can also create trust in the rest of the school and beyond, that this is a valuable course for the school to take that will benefit everyone.

One of the most effective ways of constructing such a foundation is to carry out an arts audit, as we describe in Chapter 3, Section 1. None of us individually has a wide or deep enough knowledge of the range of arts and cultures to draw up a whole arts curriculum policy, but a school staff, drawing on outside specialist knowledge from the LEA and local and national organisations, can so do. A whole-school arts curriculum policy is required, in the same way that every school needs, for instance, a 'Personal and Social Development Policy' and a 'Language Policy'. This book is researched and written to assist that overall view rather than just as a manual for an individual teacher.

The arts in their rich diversity are central to the culture of any society. Their place in the school is therefore very important. Just before the millennium a senior British politician in the House of Lords, Baroness Blackstone, spoke for us when she declared:

> *The arts are an essential component of any civilised society. In an age of uncertainty about our values, they can provide powerful forms of self-identity and communication for individuals and for the nation as a whole.*

She emphasised the crucial two-way relationship, stressing that the arts should be placed:

> *... where they properly belong at the heart of education. Arts and education feed each other. Schools and colleges are the sources of both the artists and the audiences of the future.*

(Blackstone, 1997)

2 THE RANGE OF THE ARTS

2.1 Planning breadth and depth

The school's arts curriculum should include a full range of genres, forms, cultures, and periods. That ambition is not easy to realise. Selection is necessary for reasons of time, of course, but should be carefully made from the full conspectus. Our inheritance of school curriculum tradition is very patchy, with massive gaps in each of the three.

A school firstly has to consider what it means by 'the arts'. That sounds simple, but is not quite straightforward: fashions tend to highlight certain arts and play down others at certain times. In schools this is also true. For instance, for many years dance was a minority art, virtually for girls only. The media arts, television and photography, were rarely adequately included. Similarly, architecture has been very rarely taught. Yet architecture is one of the clearest manifestations of the cultures of the globe and one to which we should address the pupils' eyes.

There are often very simple explanations that we can give our youngsters, using slides and displays, for example on the structured shapes and surface patterns in Islamic architecture. North Westminster Community School has an anthology of building materials in the playground –'The RTZ Geological Garden'– just as there may be an anthology of poetry in a library. It is a wall made up not only of local materials, such as limestone, but also of sedimentary, metamorphic, and igneous stone from more distant places, that can be looked at and touched.

The overall plan should include (in alphabetical order): architecture, ceramics, dance (for all, including boys), drama (in a range of styles, periods, and genres), graphic design, literature, media, music, products (or artefacts) such as furniture, sculpture, television, textiles, typography and book design and the visual arts.

Period and class

Within cultures, different periods and classes need representation. There has been in the past an attempt by some well meaning UK teachers to keep the so-called 'elite' arts (for example Russian-derived classical ballet or the eighteenth-century oil painting) from working-class children. For many years the cultural range experienced by most children has been limited by our class prejudices. Some pundits, with the intention of being egalitarian, had a deterministic view of the possible range of taste, and capacity to be educated, of our children. Here is an actual quote about art teaching:

> It is an unwarranted imposition of the arbitrary taste of the upper classes on working class pupils, who would therefore be led to disvalue their own cultural forms.

Many cultures had a far greater inter-penetrability than this allows. For instance, in the UK the music hall up to the mid-1950s brought periods and styles together. A mill girl in Lancashire who had left school at twelve in the early years of this century played Haydn and Schubert in a 'Ladies' Mandolin Band'. Her successors suffered from some teachers' inverted snobbery that kept the classics away.

An important foundation is to present the full range of the local tradition, as to do so opens up the diversity of arts. A school in the UK should feature the Elizabethan lute song, medieval plainsong, eighteenth-century verse, Yeats' plays, and vernacular timber architecture if it is to be ready for the range of the world's cultures – and if it is to see them as dynamic also.

Paradoxically, a good exploration of local traditions illuminates world cultures. Asian musical traditions and European ones have similar roots and this can be musically demonstrated. In Japan, the mask tradition has ancient Chinese roots. The masks used in the Gigaku dance-drama are not only the first historic masks used in Japan but are among the oldest surviving examples of masks in the entire world.

Our children have an entitlement to a range of genre, cultures, and periods. Time, resources, and knowledge are limited, and we have to be judicious in our selection. Yet the child of the future should have a wide set of experiences for our intercultural, eclectic world.

2.2 The intercultural aspects

The arts curriculum should include a range of cultural traditions. The eras when people knew only of their own age has largely gone. In

Germany in the nineteenth century, Felix Mendelssohn had never heard a performance of Bach's *Mass in B Minor*. The taste of a place and a period was far more restricted, and also more unified.

Ours is the age of eclecticism. Never before has human taste and flexibility combined with technological and public performance and display possibilities to allow responsive access to such a wide range of work. Poetry crossed the world and the eras a long time ago. Now dance, theatre, the visual arts, and even sculpture are intellectually, aesthetically, and physically accessible.

Pupils should be entitled to a complementary triple set of perspectives. Do not let us over-emphasise one alone. All our pupils are:

- members of families with their own cultural inheritance;
- they live in a part of the world which has its own local cultural traditions;
- further, they are people of the world, who should have access to a sample of world cultures.

Until this age of population mobility there has never been such an international, 'village of the world' perspective. Conversely, we have never had such respect for and love of roots. In our age of eclecticism, our pupils are entitled to the overlapping focuses of:

- the local traditions;
- their family inheritance;
- the international conspectus.

The middle focus requires a school to pay especial attention to the cultural tradition of the different pupils in the school. In many urban schools the African, Afro-Caribbean, Bangladeshi, Arabic, and Chinese traditions all need featuring. That is definitely not, however, to accept that such cultures should be featured only for the benefit of pupils from those cultural backgrounds. That would be what could be called 'proportio-centricism'– basing the range of cultures on the range of pupils in the school.

The 'family inheritance' definitely needs weaving strongly in. Not to give Bangladeshi pupils, for instance, an understanding of the Bangla traditions in the arts or a pupil of African heritage a knowledge of African ceramics, visual arts, literature, or dance would be to deny them a major aspect of their roots. On the other hand, the third focus is also every pupil's right – the international conspectus. Indeed, it is very significant to include some 'equi-distant' cultures – those that are not linked with any pupil in the school. For instance, even multi-ethnic schools usually have no pupils of Maori heritage, and to feature some aspects of Maori music and visual arts speaks equally to all. The virtually mono-ethnic schools of the UK require as wide a range under that third focus as any multi-ethnic school, although they have been further from it.

Japanese culture is among the least featured in schools. In some ways this is strange as the direct, brief, stylised story-telling of the Noh play speaks directly to all children, Japanese music is particularly accessible with its pulsating rhythm and pentatonic scales, and pupils love the direct power of the masks. An organisation called Musicworks carried a powerful scheme for a Year Four assembly derived from a Noh play, *The Ferryman*, and this was enjoyed by all.

The cultural exchanges across the Commonwealth are of particular significance to UK schools, and reflect the spirit of cherishing both one's own cultural heritage and that of others. The Commonwealth Secretary-General, launching the e.Commonwealth.net at the Commonwealth Institute in 2000, said:

> *We must all strive to ensure that, in this new century, the Commonwealth builds on its acknowledged record of promoting respect and tolerance among its magnificent diversity of cultures and traditions. 'Unity in diversity' may be a tired cliché for some – but for the Commonwealth it has real meaning.*
>
> (HE Rt Hon Don McKinnon, 10 April, 2000)

Some arts are for technical and physical reasons more difficult to show. Dance is one example, and for different reasons architecture. It is logistically difficult to bring a range of dance performers into school. A good quality, same-size colour reproduction of a painting is virtually the same as the original, but photographs of architecture in other cultures are both harder to obtain and less effective evocations.

Literature from a range of cultures is from the earliest primary years through to the final years of schooling both powerful in its impact and readily accessible through anthologies. The short story is a particularly effective form for cross-cultural explorations. You can study stories from Asia, Africa, China, Japan, and Europe in the English language. The anthology *Global Tales* is studied in schools literally across the world, and the contents make the point:

The intercultural aspects   23

> **FOCUS ON PLOT:** R. K. Narayan, (India) *An Astrologer's Day;*
> Karl Sealy, (Barbados) *The Pieces of Silver*
>
> **FOCUS ON CHARACTER:** R. K. Narayan, (India) *Crime and Punishment;*
> Nancy Chong, (Canadian-Chinese) *Warrior Woman and The Easter Hat*
>
> **FOCUS ON SETTING:** Oodgeroo Nunukul, (Stradbroke Island off the Queensland coast) *Kill to Eat;*
> Marion Strachan, (Wales) *What Do You Do in Winter?;*
> Mikhail Bulgakov, (Kiev in the Ukraine) *The Steel Windpipe*
>
> **FOCUS ON CONTEXT:** Mildred D. Taylor, (USA) *The Gold Cadillac;*
> Beverley Naidoo, (South Africa) *Poinsettias;*
> Ken Saro-Wiwa, (Ogoni-Nigeria) *Robert and the Dog;*
> E. B. Dongala, (Congo) *The Man*
>
> **FOCUS ON LANGUAGE:** Julius Lester, (Missouri, USA) *Why Apes Look Like People;*
> Alecia McKenzie, (Jamaica) *Full Stop;*
> Millie Murray, (Jamaican-UK) *The Escape*
>
> **FOCUS ON THEME:** Anita Desai, (Bengali-German) *Circus Cat Alley Cat;*
> Bernard MacLaverty, (Ireland) *More Than Just a Disease*

(Donovan, et al, 1997)

Similarly, quite simple, straightforward poetry can take us across eras and cultures. The fear of loss on returning home is understood by all. Inner-London twelve-year-olds, for instance, strongly respond to this short Chinese poem of twelve hundred years ago, one of those which perfected the then-new style of 'chüeh-chü' poem:

> *Crossing the Han River*
> by Sung Chih-Wên (660–710)
>
> Beyond the mountain there came no tidings and letters;
> Winter passed, and then went Spring.
> As I near my village my heart grows more afraid,
> And I dare not inquire of those that come to meet me.
>
> (Kotewall & Smith, 1968, p.12)

It speaks today in England as strongly as it did in China.

In comparing cultures we see that things can be both very alike, and yet very different. For instance, the decorative carving of precious stones across continents and across centuries reveals both similarities and contrasts. Jade has occupied the same position in Chinese culture as have gold and precious stones, such as rubies and diamonds, in the West. It was used for sacred objects, for treasure, and for decoration and ornament. Yet at first sight it is rather an unassuming stone. The subtle shades of creamy white and pale green were preferred and pieces have to be handled for the translucency and soft polish to be fully appreciated. What do young people think of it? How do they react today?

Never in the history of the world has there been such world-wide knowledge and connection. This is true for major political issues as well as trivial matters. But the paradox is that there is also a greater feeling for cherishing roots, and the particular than we have ever had before. Indeed, there is a new word 'retrophilia', which means the love of going backwards. We all care about who we are, and who we are depends upon who our ancestors were and who our families were. The overriding issue is how we can help our pupils balance world knowledge with this depth of understanding of roots.

Many of the 'either/or' arguments miss the point: the child of Chinese or Bangladeshi background in the UK needs both the western traditions and the Chinese or Bangladeshi roots. They illuminate each other and do not conflict. A black British pupil who is denied access to Beowulf, Shakespeare, Crabbe, and Pope is being as badly treated as a white monolingual Anglophone who is denied access to Asian, Pacific, or Chinese literature. A policy that replaces Euro-centricism with proportio-centrism (ethnic percentage representation) has not got the multicultural or intercultural balance.

Islamic art is perhaps most accessible through the pictures most people have seen of the Taj Mahal, or the architecture of Moorish Spain or North Africa. However, even pupils of Islamic faith who have been brought up in the UK are likely to be sadly limited in the range of Islam's art they are likely to know. To those with no family heritage of Islamic culture, examples of its arts often seem 'strange' or 'distant'. Few understand the inter-cultural relationships. For example, the apparently very 'English' William Morris of the European 'Arts and Crafts' movement worked aspects of Islamic principles and patterns into his designs.

In all its manifestations Islamic art is built around three themes that link with Western arts but are given a much more powerful place: geometrical patterns, natural forms (often in abstract versions), and calligraphy. Calligraphy has had moments of importance in Western aesthetics, from Roman stonework to the Arts and Crafts movement, but the Islamic focus is virtually incomparable. Because of the belief that the Qu'ran was revealed to the Prophet in the Arabic tongue and written in Arabic script, the Arab peoples reformed this script for precision and beautified it to be worthy of the renditions. Geometry is the core of

Islamic patterns and is closely derived from the cosmological approach of Greek geometry. Young people find it very interesting to have the great geometry embodied in Islamic design explained and demonstrated.

We need to remember that a cross-cultural approach to the arts involves a variety of *forms* as well as heritage. Too much of multicultural education in the arts is multicultural only in theme and human interest, and not in the artistic and cultural conventions. This is particularly true in literature. Most literatures in English (or in forms and dialects of English) start with the poem and move to the short story. For instance, that great outpouring of Caribbean short stories from the fifties onwards, a marvellous body of literature, uses a Euro-centric art *form* for Caribbean *themes*. There is nothing wrong in that at all, but we are keeping out the non-European art forms. This is why the Japanese Noh play and Indian drama, which are not basically narrative-focused, may seem alien. 'What happens next?' is the narrative-addict's fix. But that does not belong to many of the art forms of the world. You did not go to a Greek drama to know what would happen to Medea, just as you did not go to a European medieval mystery play to know what was going to happen to the chief character.

Bertolt Brecht, the German playwright, is a good way in to non-narrative drama. Pupils should recognise the contrasts and similarities between the Chinese theatre, the Japanese Noh play, the work of the Irish writer W. B. Yeats, and a few televised non-naturalistic, 'stylised' forms of drama, for instance, the S4C *Animated Tales of Shakespeare*.

These planning ideals are true for any school, certainly a mono-ethnic one. The ambition is considerably helped in the UK, however, by our country's diversity. As a recent report stressed:

> Britain has the largest population of young people in Europe from culturally diverse backgrounds, an asset that gives a greater opportunity than elsewhere in Europe for change.
>
> (Williams and Willson, 1999, p.8)

Far from there being a tension between the 'multicultural' and 'the local', there is a strong inter-cultural relationship.

2.3 The art forms

i. Introduction

For most schools, art courses are separated by the names of major art forms. This list was given additional rigidity by *The Education Reform Act 1988*, which remains the basis of the statutory regulations for the school curriculum. Although one of the authors of this book led a deputation to the then Select Committee to include 'the Arts', the suggestion was turned down. Instead, the Act retained 'Art' and 'Music', with 'Drama' included in the statutory orders for 'English' and 'Dance' included under 'Physical Education'. The general impression is that 'the arts' in schools have to follow the nomenclature of the Acts, and the full range of the arts is rarely covered.

Of course, the philosophy and semantics of discussions about 'arts' have never been entirely agreed: for instance, When is civil engineering architecture? When is ceramics sculpture? When is embroidery textiles? The very phrase 'the arts and crafts' illustrates the semantic and philosophical difficulty: When is a 'craft' not an 'art'? Where do we place and how do we define typography, ceramics, woodwork, recitation, and designing clothes?

The philosophy of this book is that secondary school pupils should be introduced to the broadest range of art forms, and that a school has to review the statutory regulations fully and deeply (not getting caught by the 'subject' labels of those orders). Only then can it plan what the full range of art forms should include. This range can be classified in various ways, but should be all-embracing. How the school 'delivers' the teaching cannot be uniform across secondary schools, for courses will very obviously have different combinations of the arts, and the contribution of 'non-arts' courses is important. However, the school should first have an overview 'arts curriculum' planned as a comprehensive view of all aspects of all the arts. The content of the then separated courses is then derived from that overview.

In this chapter, therefore, we shall rapidly scan different aspects of the arts to help in the planning of a whole-school arts curriculum.

ii Architecture

There is much to be proud about the architecture of schools since World War II (as well as many dismal nonentities of weak design), but we should be ashamed of the place architecture has in the curriculum. Very few pupils are taught how to look at a building. If the pupil is lucky, a few monuments of the past will be considered briefly, but virtually never the buildings of the local community, or even the school itself. Yet to understand a culture one has to understand its architecture, whether we are talking about the Hausa architecture of Nigeria, or the Roman memories in eighteenth-century London. The QCA specification of the Design and Technology curriculum in its 45 pages has not a single mention of architecture or buildings.

It is almost as if there has been a deliberate campaign to keep architecture out of schools. For instance, a frequently used Maths curriculum scheme in London has a unit on Aristotle's 'golden mean'. A photograph of the Parthenon has no caption and there is no explanation of the relationship between that building's columns and the geometry. In the centre of London local pupils will abstractly calculate the dimensions of the golden mean, but very rarely look at the first-floor windows of local eighteenth-century houses to see those calculations in brick and plaster echoing our classical inheritance.

The materials considered in Design Technology lessons conspicuously ignore those of significance in building. Plastic, metal, and wood are there, but brick is kept away from school children even when they are studying Tudor life. Ferroconcrete, that ubiquitous material of the second half of the last century, is barely mentioned. There is no study of its qualities, why it is used, or how it affects the structure patterns of a building. The same is true of all basic structural elements. Although GCSE students study bridge structures in their science course, most pupils are never asked to consider the structure of an actual building. They have no concept of 'load-bearing' or of 'frame'. We have found that most fourteen-year-olds sitting in a ferroconcrete frame building, with the pillars clearly in view, are baffled when asked: 'What holds this building up?' 'Rocks', 'stone', or 'bricks' are the most common answers. Would we accept such ignorance in any other 'everyday' field?

In the arts and technology the stress on practical activity has been perverted so that pupils 'have been so busy *doing* that they have had no time for *seeing*'. In researching, David Hargreaves noted the teacher 'undertook art appreciation only incidentally in the course of ordinary lessons' (1983, p.133). There has been a fear that teachers are not teaching if their pupils are '*just* looking'. This is dubbed as 'passive', with 'spectator' as a pejorative word and 'appreciation' an almost forgotten one. The emphasis on designing and *making* in technology has almost completely excluded the designing of articles that cannot be made because of their complexity, materials, or scale. The school workbench has become a curriculum tyrant: if something cannot be made on one, it should not be learnt about! Thus buildings are out.

As we have described, there has been a considerable cultural widening of the range of experiences and studies in dance, music, literature, and the visual arts. This multicultural variety has not penetrated the technology curriculum, despite excellent work by the Commonwealth Institute. The secondary curriculum should include the architectures of a variety of cultures. The Head of Visual Arts at North Westminster

Community School found that a brief study of African building helped younger secondary pupils *see* their familiar architectural surroundings afresh. An in-depth study of one African region, *Hausa Architecture*, is an excellent source for a unit for thirteen-year-olds (Moughtin, 1995).

The extent of the failure to see even what is around the teachers and the pupils is shocking. Woodberry Down School was a successful North London secondary school with a Craft, Design, and Technology Department. The workshops were spanned by an impressive range of unusually long Vierendeel beams, yet the pupils learning design underneath them were apparently never taught to analyse them. They learnt *under* them but not *from* them.

Similarly, for 30 years pupils were taught in Leonard Manasseh's Rutherford School off the Edgware Road. Its basic structure of load-bearing window mullions, from ground to roof line at 3'8½' intervals, gives the long building its character, with windows and panels below them reading as a continuous vertical strip. It is also an anthology of interesting structural features, with the pyramid of the assembly-hall roof almost jokingly echoed by an *inverted* pyramid for the water tank above the main flat roof. The use of materials is both restrained and rich, with a marvellous foyer walled in Carrara marble, an assembly hall in fine hardwood, and corridors in Ruabon tiles. Three thousand secondary pupils had been taught in that building: but how many had been taught to look at the building itself? Pupils have been seen in Science learning about concrete by mixing it in beakers – without being led to consider the concrete they were standing on or that of the mullions through which the sun was shining.

Every school should develop a whole-school curriculum plan covering the built environment. We need to look to architects' organisations to build on the RIBA's work and publish model curriculum policies. Publishers need to produce books and wall charts for pupils. *In Our Street*, by the City of Westminster Arts Council shows how the Art requirements of National Curriculum legislation could be used to investigate local buildings, starting with such simple but crucial activities as 'observation and discussion of typical houses in the street'.

An impressive number of schools are 'building' buildings into the arts curriculum. This includes visits to study completed buildings of all periods, the study of buildings still under construction, visits by architects and civil engineers, and displays of pictures that teach by their juxtapositions of form, material, and function. Some schools have built collections of bricks, free-standing ferroconcrete pillars with the steel rods half-exposed, and wall displays of wood joints.

There is an urban design aspect of 'Citizenship', although the aesthetic element is sometimes forgotten. Yet the National Curriculum overall handbooks state: 'The school curriculum . . . should develop [in pupils] an awareness and an understanding of, and respect for, the environments in which they live.' (DfEE and QCA, 1999, primary and secondary, p.11) This should include all aspects of architecture – including street design. There is a continuum from the functional aspects of urban development, from drains to traffic movement to artistic details, from the forms of buildings to their facades. The organisation Streetwise (see the Appendix) is very helpful to schools with its journal and consultation facilities. Indeed, its book for young people, *Investigating Shopping*, is a history of shops with a strong artistic content (Montford, 1993).

The Geography requirements of the National Curriculum for England require Key Stage 2 pupils 'to identify how and why places change *[for example, through the closure of shops or building of new houses, through conservation projects]* and how they may change in the future *[for example, through an increase in traffic or an influx of tourists]*' (*The National Curriculum, Handbook for primary teachers*, 1999, p.113). The Key Stage 3 requirements virtually repeat that.

Yet most children are brought up in our society with very little that leads them to look at and consider such everyday structural things as different woods and the joints in wood. They are not asked to look at the pitch of roofs, and to consider that roofs were steeply pitched when they were thatched to throw off the rain, but the pitch went shallow when the canal age brought slate across the country. They are rarely asked to look at a wall and ask if the bricks are load bearing or in-filling to a frame construction.

The brick is one of the least taught aspects of life, and hardly a child has been asked to think about its size, or to hold one, or to look at the joints. The Tudor period taught in Key Stage 2 is usually without a mention of bricks or chimneys and their contribution to the art of architecture. The significance of the 1571 Act of Parliament defining brick sizes is left out. The difference between wrought iron and cast iron is rarely considered, a point of considerable aesthetic significance. Ferroconcrete is rarely mentioned. The different stones used in building are not linked to the geology taught. The vocabulary of the construction world, and the concepts embodied in those terms, is omitted from most schools – and thus thinking about and the reading of architecture is not facilitated.

A number of existing primary schools are in three-storey 'Board' schools, built by the School Boards set up by the 1870 Education Act. The central halls on the ground and first floor frequently have their 'I' beams open to inspection, but millions of children have sat on the floor for assemblies day after day in the last century and not been asked to look up at the beams and ponder how they work as they do. This is an important but simple structural point that could easily be explained to the young pupil.

A physics teacher teaching fifteen-year-olds about stresses and bridge building did not mention the bridges within two or three minutes' walk of the school that demonstrate arch construction and suspension, nor touch on the aesthetic aspect of bridge structure.

There have been some very helpful teaching materials, but not many. A very practical one, both modest and simple, was published by the Geography Teachers' Centre in the City of London in 1986 'to encourage teachers and children to look at the built environment with a new and enquiring eye' (Dunkley and Maddams, 1986, p.3).

We should teach pupils from the youngest ages to observe and to speculate: 'Why is that building as it is, and how could it have been otherwise?' Pupils can begin to understand the influence of location, materials, function, economics, and available technology. Some years ago an initiative was taken by the mining company RTZ, who mounted a series of architectural walks for school-children growing out of their music festival at St James' Piccadilly. It took in, for instance, St James's Square, Lutyens' Midland Bank, Burlington House, Cullum and Nightingale's new mews house, and Boodles' Club. Very clear teachers' notes and an excellently designed pupils' leaflet was produced by a retired teacher, Jack Whitehead (1993).

Perhaps Leonardo da Vinci's phrase should be part of every school curriculum: *'Sempire, videre'*, balancing the need to teach *how* to see with the learning that comes *from* educated looking. The Design Technology course should feature specific built-environment units and History, Geography, and Art should have relevant references to the architecture of a place, a period, and a culture.

▬ iii Ceramics

In so many subtle ways 'pottery' has been both one of the most significant art/crafts and one of the least prominent. William Morris's great ideal of a craftsperson both designing and making a complete object from raw materials to the final product has been most often achieved in ceramics. In a complementary way, John Ruskin's ideas of 'the beauty of imperfection' was more easily and fully realised in ceramics than in other media. In fact, 'pottery' had an early and fairly prominent place in British education. The *Handbook of Suggestions* for Elementary Schools in 1937 declared:

> *Pottery – few crafts provide so rich a background of tradition as Pottery, and it is certainly one of the most valuable in providing a well balanced training in skill and in promoting appreciation of form, colour and texture.*

However, the same *Handbook* then went on to say:

> *While, however, most schools can provide for some elementary experience of the craft, few are able to provide the complete equipment which is necessary in order to get the best results.*
>
> (Board of Education, 1937, p.261)

Sadly, this is still true today. A relatively small number of secondary schools have general introductions with clay, wheel, glaze, and kiln for all Key Stage 3 pupils and specialised continuity. Some primary schools have introductory sessions, and there are schools with a wide and continuous coverage. However, ceramics is one of the least well covered arts in schools. This is partly because the mixing, moulding, glazing, and firing sequence is difficult in equipment and classroom activity terms.

Also, the admirable practical emphasis of actually handling and directly making almost removes the pure appreciative element. Thus, very few pupils have access to the history and cultural forms of the ceramic art. For instance, the British Leach tradition of hand-cast and decorated pottery in a 1920s art form derived from the Orient is rarely introduced to pupils. Very few pupils have had a chance to observe, think about, and judge the range of twentieth-century pottery, and its relationship with the traditions of other cultures. For instance, many schools proud of their multicultural traditions have made no introduction to Zambian pottery. Yet:

> *Zambia has a wide and varied tradition of pottery, going back many centuries. Apart from the pottery used from day to day, there is also an interesting variety of richly decorated pots and figurines for important occasions like initiation ceremonies and weddings, and special pots which are made for high-ranking people.*
>
> (Lorenz, 1989, p.1)

The appreciative aspect of ceramics faces the obvious problem of access – pupils cannot always experience the feel as well as the look of fine ceramics for practical reasons, and reproductions, such as can be successfully made for most forms of visual arts, from oils to lithographs, are not available. The real objects are delicate and difficult to obtain and handle. Displays in proper display cabinets may be possible but hard to arrange.

Some hands-on experience should be included in the primary years, no doubt without glazing in most cases, and Key Stage 3 should include some kiln-baked pottery work. Only a few schools will be able to follow this into Key Stage 4. After-hours volunteer sessions should be made available if at all possible. There should also be proper references in geography and history. The use of clays for tiles, bricks, and pottery is part of environmental education. The place of pottery in human and industrial life should be included, as it should in cultural history. For instance, Key Stage National Curriculum History includes the example of Ancient Greece. The legend of Theseus and Minos should surely include Greek ceramics of the time. 'Effects of Roman settlement' should include Roman pottery.

The range of twentieth-century pottery in the UK is immense, with the great individualists still cherished: Bernard Leach, Lucie Rie, Elizabeth Fritsch and Hans Coper. Even in a school that can do a little or no kiln work, the appreciation of ceramics should be woven into one of the courses using exhibitions, slides, and the occasional handled example (available from the Crafts Council, details in Appendix 2).

iv Dance

Dance is rarely mentioned in Ofsted reports, perhaps because of the shortage of specialist inspectors. This may also have to do with the Ofsted mode of inspecting: for obvious practical reasons, only that which takes place on the few days of inspection is commented on. One county summed it up:

> In Nottinghamshire, out of 170 OFSTED reports in 1996, only three primary schools and no secondary school reports mention dance. OFSTED inspectors do not always report on everything happening in schools (e.g. dance activities). Non-specialist inspectors always comment positively on dance classes where they are found, even if it is bad teaching. This is because they do not know how to assess them. The result is a limited development of dance as an art form. Dance specialists should inspect dance lessons.

(National Advisory Committee, 1999, p.115)

We have already indicated the overall low inclusion in schools of dance. It was included in the National Curriculum, though confusingly under the 'Physical Education' heading. The evidence suggests that the first imposition of the legislation in the early nineties led to an increase in Key Stage 2, cynics saying because it was somewhat cheaper and technically easier in some primary schools than the alternatives under 'Physical Education'. Further, it is not compulsory in Key Stages 2 or 3, but one of the options. A DfEE officer confirmed in 1998 (and this still applies):

It is possible to meet the statutory requirements of the KS3 programme of study for PE without teaching Dance. A school could, for example, as a minimum provide: Games, Swimming (as the second 'full area' of activity), Gymnastic activities (Unit A), and Athletic activities (Unit A).

There are some LEAs where most primary schools have planned dance elements in the curriculum: Manchester is an outstanding example. However, Calouste Gulbenkian reported in 1980 that whilst 70% of primary schools in the country had a named teacher responsible for music, only 13% had one for dance and only 17% had any written guidelines or policy. We estimate that dance is not as often featured in schools as it should be – especially for boys in secondary schools.

It is perhaps not surprising that there is, to use the Calouste Gulbenkian phrase, a 'national ignorance of the significance of dance' (Calouste Gulbenkian, 1980, p.1). Inherited school attitudes have lingered, such as gender bias, the idea that working-class children should not have upper-class culture imposed on them, and the confusion that came from the National Curriculum listing dance under PE.

However, dance really is successful when it is taught by specialists in a strong performing arts context. It is, after all, such a fundamental mode of human expression. It relates to a whole range of cultures and period, and even the simplest gesture by an early learner can be deeply moving. It brings music and drama together; develops perceptual skills; offers ways of relating feelings, values, and expression; encourages sensitivity in relationships with others; and brings aesthetic imagination into close relationship with basic bodily movements.

Dance has enabled so many young people to bring composition, performance and audience appreciation together. There is no doubt from practical experience that it has a deeply significant place in the school curriculum, bringing creative art to the most basic human skill: that of movement.

v Drama

Drama is a key art in schools, and a wide-ranging survey of secondary schools just before the end of the twentieth century found that: 'Despite all the difficulties, drama is well established in the majority of schools and colleges.' (Miller, 1998, p.62) However, coherent planning and relating its various traditions to the whole-school curriculum can be hampered by problems of venues, equipment, staffing and time-tabling.

The basic requirements of the National Curriculum for Drama are simply set out in Key Stage 2:

To participate in a wide range of drama activities and to evaluate their own and others' contributions, pupils should be taught to:

- *create, adapt and sustain different roles, individually and in groups*
- *use character, action and narrative to convey story, themes, emotions, ideas in plays they devise and script*
- *use dramatic techniques to explore characters and issues, for example, hot seating, flashback!*
- *evaluate how they and others have contributed to the overall effectiveness of performances.*

Drama activities – the range should include:

- *improvisation and working in role*
- *scripting and performing in plays*
- *responding to performances.*

(DfEE and QCA, English, 1999, pp.23–4)

The versions for Key Stages 3 and 4 are essentially the same, though carefully elaborated. The attempt of the National Curriculum legislation of 1988 to define 'drama' within the category of 'English' should not limit the actual *school* curriculum. 'Drama' can be taught as a separate course, or within the Performing Arts (for example with Music and Dance), or in Creative Arts (plus the visual arts). Although it is unlikely, it would also be possible to put it within a course on 'Literature', and place the language aspect of National Curriculum 'English' in 'Languages'.

However, it *is* a specialism, and as the Secondary Heads Association stresses:

- *Though it may be sensible for drama to be set within an Arts Faculty, there should always be a specialist Head of Department.*
- *Drama, no less than any other subject, requires fully qualified specialist teachers.*
- *It cannot be automatically assumed that drama can be taught either within the English curriculum or by English teachers.*

(Miller, 1998, p.42)

The full range of cultural backgrounds should be included from Key Stage 2, as the concept of the 'inter-cultural' is especially important in drama. The National Curriculum 'English' specifically requires for Key Stages 3 and 4 the inclusion of 'drama, fiction and poetry by major writers from different cultures and traditions', for example Athol Fugard,

Arthur Miller, Wole Soyinka, and Tennessee Williams (DfEE and QCA, English, 1999, p.36).

We have two main strands of justification for drama in the curriculum:

- It is an essential part of the aesthetic range of the arts;
- It is a sensitive developmental and pedagogic means of working with children.

At different times the balance has been, sometimes severely, readjusted. Indeed, to a considerable extent the priority of drama in schools has less to do with its place in 'the arts' as with the stress on 'child-centred' learning and 'creative' English in the 1950s and 60s. By the end of the twentieth-century the balance was better, with the cultural, aesthetic, skills, and theatre aspects being given the lead. (In the central government's 'Schools Council' in the seventies, 'skill' was a term ruled out by the Drama Committee members!)

The school vision of 'drama' thus needs careful and complex defining, particularly as it relates to music, design, and dance.

A major survey in late 1998 argued strongly for a balanced approach to the subject:

- In the light of drama's positive impact on literacy through oracy it would be short-sighted and counter-productive to reduce curriculum time for drama in order to make room for other literacy work.
- In curriculum planning at Key Stages 3 and 4 drama should be recognised for having an essential contribution to make to academic and personal development.
- The success of extra-curricular drama should not submerge the crucial contribution that educational drama makes to pupil development. Each school should seek to have an appropriate balance between them.

(Miller, 1998, p.42–3)

HMI speaks of the value of drama from the youngest age:

There is a strong tradition in early years education for including primitive materials, such as sand, water and clay, clothes for 'dressing-up' play, and play in simulated 'home corners'. The roots of drama are all too obvious in children's play in these areas.

(Hertrich, 1998, p.46)

This HMI praises the place of drama from then onwards, and gives interesting examples of good work. He stresses that:

> Good drama in schools draws on a rich field of reference and ... any of the lessons described here might be placed on a spectrum running from drama as performance to participation in drama to gain greater control of language, enlarge vocabulary, and explore relationships and emotions.

(Hertrich, 1998 p.57)

He supports the potential contribution to Personal and Social Development, saying that schools should:

> Make explicit drama's contribution to pupils' personal, social, moral and spiritual development, and take care in exploring complex themes or 'issues' to ensure that their treatment is not superficial.

(Hertrich, 1998 p.58)

vi Film, television, and radio drama

It could be said that the least explored art form in schools, competing for this lowly status with tapestry and architecture, is the radio play. (Even the National Curriculum leaves out 'radio'.) Most pupils have left school without once having heard, read, or discussed a radio play. Whilst the range of drama forms made for film, television, and radio can be regarded as part of 'literature' and 'drama', the structural, technological, and aesthetic differences are very great, and we suggest whole-school planning should identify these related dramatic forms.

Radio plays are, of all performed drama, the form most created in the heads of the audience. A radio play has just four ingredients: voices, sounds, music, and (very importantly) silence. This focused extract from the complexity of life gives the radio play some artistic closeness to other quasi-'abstract' arts, such as sculpture (shape and posture but no movement or sound) and dance (movement but no voice). Of all art forms, this uses the strongest and most focused form of expression: sound only. Because the actors are not *seen*, the total focus on the voice is deeply evocative. With no scenery, costume, or lighting, nor description of the characters' appearances, the dialogue has to create character, carry the action forward, reveal information, and capture the listener.

The radio play now lacks the cultural impact that it had before the rise of television. Yet it can be effectively included in English courses, with a focus on scripting and drama. It is especially valuable in PSHE and Tutorial Periods to explore personal and emotional themes. The sound-only presentation encourages tutor-group discussions.

Film, television, and video recordings are also valuable media. They are virtually identical art forms, although the size of the screen affects their impact, as does using a home or public venue. Whilst the core of the art form is virtually the same as 'live theatre', the particular artistic-technical aspects need specific teaching.

What you *see* is as important as what you *hear*, and the camera 'shooting' and subsequent 'editing' are twentieth-century art skills that pupils need to be helped to understand technically and aesthetically. Pupils tend to think that actors act and the camera picks it up. That the number of cameras, their positions, and their focus is planned; and that the subsequent filmed sequences are 'cut' and 'edited' needs very detailed teaching. The naturalistic style of television and film acting and play production often makes it seem as if the visual sequence is actual 'life itself'. Pupils should understand filming techniques, such as camera angle, variations between whom you *see* and what you *hear* – for instance you might be shown a close-up of one person's face whilst hearing another person's comments. Editing and cutting are very important techniques that pupils value having explained, analysed, and reviewed. Demonstration videos are necessary, with discussions about editing in drama, news and documentary.

However the curriculum is divided into 'courses', the analytic and appreciative understanding of sound and visual production should be specifically taught and the analytic approaches reinforced in a variety of contexts – from tutorial periods to history lessons. The National Curriculum's 'English' inclusion of 'non-fiction and non-literary texts' specifies: 'media and moving image texts', including in the examples: 'television, films, video' (though oddly not radio). The artistic genre of visual and sound-only drama should be experienced, the techniques taught, and if possible, some performing participation arranged for all pupils.

vii Graphic design

Put on a CD, pick up a newspaper or book, switch on the TV, go shopping, stick a stamp on an envelope, wait at a bus-stop, go to the match or a gig. Look around you – at the advertising hoardings, at shop windows, the ticket or programme in your hand. All these different aspects of everyday life include elements of graphic design. Everything you see or touch has been designed, well or badly; they have all been created by someone thinking and working graphically.

What is graphic design? *The Encyclopaedia of Graphic Design and Designers* (Livingston, 1992) defines it as:

> [the] generic term for the activity of combining typography, illustration, photography and printing for purposes of persuasion, information, or instruction.

38 The range of the arts

Graphic design embraces illustration, packaging, and promotion. It creates the logos on your jeans, and identifies the bank you use, the garage where you fill up your car, or the tube, metro, or train company which owns the train you travel in. Graphic design is of its time, and can quickly date. Yet classic design, which transcends its time by virtue of its quality and 'fitness for purpose', readily comes back. Think of the packaging, posters, logos, or advertising that you remember well – for example at random: Startrite, Michelin, Your Country Needs You, Coca-Cola, Nike, Channel 4 and BBC identities, the Saul Bass-designed opening sequences for Hitchcock and Preminger films, album covers for the Beatles, Rolling Stones, Roxy Music and so on.

Graphic design is art itself and has influenced art movements, most notably pop art. Consider the use of graphic images by artists such as Roy Lichtenstein, Andy Warhol, and Peter Blake.

Graphic design also straddles art and technology. Some designers work on computers; others eschew the technology and work in the 'traditional' way of graphic design – the archetypal, but for many designers still very real, back of an envelope and pencil. One great British graphic designer John Gorham called them: 'My only gizmo and my mouse'.

Exploring graphic design can take us on a journey into the origins of designers' work. We can observe the way they seek to develop, plan and communicate the client's, or their own, ideas or message, and the social, historical, and economic contexts of their work. We can see what worked then and what works now in terms of the cultural and political awareness of the audience, and our ability to 'make connections'. Why do we get the message so fast? Why do we 'like' one piece of graphic design (a poster, logo, package) and not others? Why are we prompted to act (for example buy, support, laugh) on seeing one and not another?

Graphic design identifies us and identifies corporations. It enters the area of politics and the debate about globalisation and the power of brands – as set out by Naomi Klein in her book *No Logo* (2000). What is it about a design that determines whether we feel good about a company or a product? Can we admire the design of a logo but dislike the company it identifies? In short, when are we consumers and when are we citizens? And when can or cannot we be both at the same time?

Our graphic design journey therefore takes us into and across the whole curriculum in the same way that it gets us into and across the school. It is as essential as literacy and numeracy. It expresses ideas and offers new perspectives. Edward de Bono explains it this way:

> I believe that 'design' as such is grossly undervalued in our society and education – because the awful Greek gang of three led us to believe that analysis and

judgement were enough. Most of the major problems in the world will not be solved by further analysis. They need design.

(McAlhone and Stuart, 1996, p.8)

There clearly should be specific teaching of graphic design and production, as well as evaluation and appreciation, in the art course. These should be supported by the occasional consideration of posters, book jackets, and the range of printed ephemera in such courses as History, Drama, Science, Music, Media, and Literature.

viii Literature

Literature is arguably the most widely covered art in schools, the one most clearly spelled out by central government, and the only one taught to GCSE for virtually all pupils.

The National Curriculum programmes of study for English require pupils to 'read a wide range of texts independently, both for leisure and for study,' so that they 'become enthusiastic, discriminating and responsive readers, understanding layers of meaning and appreciating what they read on a critical level'. This should embrace the English literary heritage (especially Shakespeare), texts from different cultures and traditions, recent and contemporary drama, fiction and poetry, plus travel writing, reportage, personal records and viewpoints on society and writing on the natural world.

So literature is more than novels or poems or plays. It embraces, for example, the written work of psychiatrists Sigmund Freud and Carl Jung, scientists Richard Dawkins and Primo Levi, architectural writers Alec Clifton-Taylor and Deyan Sudjic, sports writers John Arlott and CLR James and naturalists Gilbert White and Richard Mabey. Literature embraces, supports and explains other art forms and other subject areas.

To some extent, and more *soto voce* than before, the National Curriculum is telling us what we should read – or at least some of what we should read. Implicit in these requirements is the notion that this is a starting point rather than a comprehensive listing. The challenge remains for the teacher, and the individual pupil, to keep asking the questions: What should I read? What should I recommend others to read?

One response is to say just read anything, but keep reading. A more rewarding response might be to find a balance between being guided in one's choice and having chance encounters, valuing their serendipitous and idiosyncratic nature: negotiating the canon (or canons) and exploring beyond that canon. Like the Knight in Chaucer's *Canterbury Tales*, one is constantly keeping appointments one never made.

A more basic question might be: why read? The answers may seem self-evident. After all, literacy is at the core of learning. But being able to read and reading literature are two identifiable elements, separate but related, in the act of literacy.

The American writer and literary critic Harold Bloom has long explored and extolled the act of reading (and more controversially, of subject matter, at least in the western canon of literature). He stresses that we read for ourselves:

> *It matters, if individuals are to retain any capacity to form their own judgments and opinions, that they continue to read for themselves. How they read, well or badly, and what they read, cannot depend wholly upon themselves, but why they read must be for and in their own interest.*
>
> (*How to Read and Why*, Bloom, Fourth Estate, 2000)

Reading literature enables us to enlarge life and to put 'more life into a time without boundaries'. We read, Bloom concludes, because we can not know enough people profoundly enough, because we need to know ourselves better and because we require knowledge, not just of ourselves and others, but of the way things are.

In this book we have stressed cultural breadth. We all inherit considerable confusion about how this affects literature: should 'English Literature' include literature from other countries? Indeed there have been many arguing against literature in translation. In the twenty-first century we are better placed to diversify. Let us consider one example.

Rabindranath Tagore warrants a significant place in the secondary schools arts curriculum. Most famous for his poetry, he also wrote fifteen plays, of which *The Post Office* in the Radice/Parvin version (Tagore Centre, 1996) is eminently suitable for secondary schools. He painted and drew two thousand pictures and sketches; composed over two thousand songs; and was an actor, singer and producer. He brings the arts together for secondary school pupils, and in so doing he brings a range of cultures together. The story poem *A Half Acre of Land* particularly speaks to Key Stage 3 pupils. The moving short poem *Unending Love* in the Tagore Centre collection *This World is Beautiful* is specially collated for young readers. William Radice's *Selected Poems* (Penguin, 1985) is a marvellously wide-ranging collection, with helpful notes. Tagore also wrote over ninety stories. The useful school collection *Asian Stories* (Bhinda, 1992) includes the delightful *The Babus of Nayanjore*.

The current English 'teaching requirements' for Key Stages 3 and 4 include drama, fiction and poetry by major writers from different cultures and traditions. One of the seven poets suggested is Tagore, the only Asian included. His poetry is therefore key for the multicultural English curriculum. Whilst inseparable from his Bengali background, Tagore is a part of the whole world. William Radice speaks powerfully of his vision: 'The passion and dignity of Tagore's idealism; the sense of horror at human evil; a tragic feeling of fairness and isolation from the world as it is actually run by professional men; and a profound feeling of nearness to the world of the spirit' (Tagore, 1985, p.30).

ix Media (including newspapers and advertisements)

In this era, young people significantly develop their concepts of culture and creativity through representations on television and, to a lesser extent, radio and newspapers. The National Curriculum requirements initially included a paragraph on media under the planning division called 'English'. In fact, as a British Board of Film Classification research study showed, Ofsted reports very rarely include any reference to media study. It is our impression that this aspect of the external requirements on the school curriculum is not being properly covered in a significant number of schools.

Pupils should be introduced to a wide range of media, for example magazines, newspapers, radio, television, film. They should be given opportunities to analyse and evaluate such material, which should be of high quality and represent a range of forms and purposes, with different structural and presentational devices.

No English course would be complete today without the integration of the newer media into the classroom consideration. Last night's television soap and today's newspaper must take their place in the continuum that ranges from the most trivial of reading matter to major literature. As in many rich aspects of life, it is difficult and often artificial to categorise and divide. Newspapers and magazines are included in 'reading ... of ... non-fiction and non-literary texts' in the English division of the national requirements for the school curriculum.

Since the establishment of the Teacher Training Agency, the place of 'Media' in initial training of teachers has been fairly well defined:

> *Trainees must be taught how to introduce pupils to the analysis and composition of the media within the pupils' National Curriculum for English, including newspapers, television and film through activities which:*
>
> a *demonstrate some of the ways in which meaning is presented by the media and consider how form, layout and presentation contribute to impact and persuasion;*
>
> b *teach about institutions that produce media and require pupils to evaluate the messages and values communicated by the media;*
>
> c *require pupils to consider the ways in which audiences and readers choose and respond to media.*
>
> (*Initial Teacher Training*, Annex F, 1998, p.10)

The broad coverage of 'Media and moving image texts' under 'Reading' in 'English' in National Curriculum Key Stages 3 and 4 is sound and necessary, though we doubt if it has been fully woven into the work of most schools:

> **Media and moving image texts**
> *Pupils should be taught:*
>
> a *how meaning is conveyed in texts that include print, images and sometimes sounds*
>
> b *how choice of form, layout and presentation contribute to effect [for example, font, caption, illustration in printed text, sequencing, framing, soundtrack in moving image text]*
>
> c *how the nature and purpose of media products influence content and meaning [for example, selection of stories for a front page or news broadcast]*
>
> d *how audiences and readers choose and respond to media.*
>
> *The range should include:*
>
> a *literary non-fiction*
> b *print and ICT-based information and reference texts*
> c *media and moving image texts [for example newspapers, magazines, advertisements, television, films, videos].*
>
> (DfEE and QCA, 1999, pp.50–1)

The 'drama' aspects of those headings has been covered in section vi.

For the many pupils unfamiliar with the making of a television programme, the teacher must point out that even the simplest programme represents a pooling of effort and is the culmination of a complex, co-operative venture. The actual process of creating with television provides the children with numerous opportunities for rehearsing many different kinds of language. At the same time, they are learning for themselves some of the unexplored potential of the medium that culturally dominates so many people's lives.

The choice of what *is* news, which aspect will be 'headlined', and which tone will be used are the key questions for all of us 'reading' the news whether in print, television, or sound. These analytic skills have to be taught and practised.

By the consideration of actual examples, weighing word against word, headline against headline, and story against story (often for this purpose reproduced anonymously in print or typescript) the reader is encouraged to read more widely and to create her or his own standards. The core of the work is the consideration of two reports of the same event. The teacher is not in the position of a censor, but of a questioner asking: 'Well, which is the more convincing and more interesting of the two?'

The majority of pupils face a number of difficulties that prevent their full use and understanding of the newspaper:

- They have read very few different papers;
- Of the papers they have seen, they have read only a few parts;
- Their knowledge of the actual range of news is meagre;
- They accept that 'news' = 'reality' because they lack understanding of editorial methods;
- Their small vocabularies hamper reading of fuller reports.

It is a good exercise to take the headlines of three or four papers and have the class compare them. It is sometimes worth taking a news story from the past, thus with no contemporary reference, and with that distant view have the pupils analyse the difference. The following exercise is always a good one. In 1964 the Labour party won the election, Harold Wilson became Prime Minister, and Edward Heath Leader of the Opposition. At the end of that parliament there was a critical debate with the opposition pushing a 'no confidence' motion. Three versions, each using accurate facts but shaping them:

> Labour win by 13 after Commons storm
> WILSON AND HEATH CLASH –
> FACE TO FACE
>
> Two minutes to go and Premier is shouted down
> WILSON RATTLED IN FIRST HEATH CLASH
>
> PRIME MINISTER BEATS MR. HEATH TO PUNCH
> 'No confidence' motion lost by 13 votes

Individual words can be compared in actual phrases describing the same detail.

a *mob* of youths	a *crowd* of youths
the *problem*	the *riddle*
the senior administration *quits*	the senior administration *resigns*
the boy was *brought before* the court	the boy was *hauled* into court

Whole newspaper analyses of proportion of space and emphasis on different aspects should also be undertaken.

The newspaper organisation needs explaining. In the popular mind, the reporter tends to be over-emphasised, and the departmental editors overlooked. The importance of the sub-editor also needs clarifying.

Photographic analysis and how press photographers work is also important. It is noticeable when, for instance, a local newspaper photographer visits a school (a most interesting *lesson*) how surprised the pupil observers or participants are at the artificiality of the compressed grouping the photographer requires and the number of shots attempted.

Many readers tend to see the photograph as printed as if it were the actual event. How the photographer gets to be there, arranges that view, and chooses that angle needs discussing – and a selection of similar pictures should be compared. Specially devised shots of, say, the school classroom can be studied to demonstrate how different shots can give a completely different impression. Similarly, a wide-angled shot of a crowd and a close-up of one angry face in that very crowd can be contrasted. Finally, the in-house photo-editor who 'crops' the pictures should be included, with pairs or trios of the same picture cropped differently compared.

Many of the same techniques are used to enable pupils to have an analytic, objective approach to advertisements. Advertisements are an inescapable part of our environment, providing our major experience of graphic design, a sizeable proportion of our reading matter, and a repeated evocation of the aims and standards of society. We can teach objective discrimination by the positive approach of the whole education, particularly in considering language, literature, and art. In addition to that, pupils need training in design and craftsmanship in workshop and home economic rooms. The genuine and accurate use of language in a poem, the experience of the reality of personal relations in a story, the enjoyment of an unsentimental painting – these are experiences that help one to recognise sentimentality, exaggeration, and irrelevance when they are used in advertising.

When a more direct approach is needed, a folder of comparative examples will be found useful. The emphasis is less on 'consumer protection' and the 'best buy' (important as these are), but more on how to judge a good or bad advertisement in terms of the means it uses and the reactions it produces.

Pupils can be given or can prepare for themselves questions to use with ads put before them in the class or ones they have collected themselves. For example:

- Where did the advertisement appear?
- Who is likely to see it, many people or only certain sorts of people? What type of audience has the advertiser in mind?
- What is design?
- Is the product illustrated so as to give the consumer a true idea of its appearance?
- What are the key words, and what ideas do they bring to mind?
- What information would the average consumer require to know about this product?
- What information is actually given? Is this adequate, relevant, accurate?
- Are any special claims made for the product?
- How could they be checked?
- Is the product being linked to any particular way of life?
- What is the main line of appeal?
- Is it a sensible appeal for this product?
- Is it a fair means of persuasion?

It is important that both newspapers and advertisements are not presented to the pupils only in a negative frame. For instance, it is valuable to collect and display advertisements for charity and discuss both their merits and problems, considering their links with personal and social aspects of the curriculum. Pupils can be asked to consider such qualities as:

- Are the skills of graphic designers and copy-writers put to the best use in the advertising industry, or are there other, socially more important, tasks that these people could do?
- Is it right that potentially harmful habits such as smoking and drinking should be advertised at all?
- Is it a good thing that important emotions, such as maternal feeling or sexual love, should be used to sell?
- Should advertisements be made to appeal to children?

In all aspects of media work, the curriculum is enabling the pupil to understand, judge, and appreciate a wider range of examples and to be an independent, sensitive judge. Newspapers and advertisements are forms of art and the same evaluative, appreciative knowledge and skills are required.

x Music

The debate about the 'transfer' effects of engaging in or with music is well known. Doing music can make you better at maths or modern languages or logical thinking. The jury is still out on what is often called the 'Mozart effect', whereby listening to music by Mozart is found to have a positive impact on Maths ability.

But we should not ignore the wider benefits that listening to, playing, and understanding music can give us. The NFER study *Arts Education in Secondary Schools: effects and effectiveness* (Harland, et al, 2000) documents heightened senses of enjoyment and fulfilment; improved knowledge and skills – technical, expressive, creative; and advances in personal and social development. Projects carried out by the National Foundation for Youth Music are resulting in increased self-confidence, commitment, and, crucially, enjoyment in the young people involved in playing and singing – or just taking part.

Music professor Nicholas Cook, in his absorbing book *Music: a very short introduction* (1998) writes of music being a 'means of insight into other cultures [and] of negotiating cultural identity'. It can also be a means to understand different strands within a single culture. He emphasises the many ways that music can inform, delight, and persuade, both explicitly and 'secretly' through the promotional uses of music in adverts and films – what he calls 'the ultimate hidden persuader'. He concludes:

That is why, in the end, it is not just musicologists who need to acquire a critical orientation. As Adorno clearly understood, critical theory omits music at its peril; music has unique powers as an agent of ideology. We need to understand its working, its charms, both to protect ourselves against them and, paradoxically, to enjoy them to the full. And in order to do that, we need to be able not just to hear music but to read it too: not in literal, notational terms, to be sure, but for its significance as an intrinsic part of culture, of society, of you and me.

(Cook, 1998, p.129)

All this gives schools good reason to develop a music environment. Unfortunately, in practical terms, music is often seen as a difficult subject to work into the school day. Music often happens outside school timetable hours and involves too few pupils on a regular basis. However, this is motivating many music services, individual music teachers, and the more innovative orchestras, ensembles, and professional musicians to seek ways of collaborating with schools. This will extend the reach of 'hands-on' music provision in terms of numbers, musical genres and cultural traditions. It also requires the active involvement of other subject teachers with an interest or skill in music.

The institutions with which such collaborations can be set up include hospitals, prisons, workplaces, and care settings. The technological developments of music equipment give many more young people the chance to write, rehearse, and record their own music.

One example of such partnership involved pupils from Leiston High School in Suffolk and young offenders at the nearby Carlford Unit of Hollesley Bay prison. The group of young offenders spent two weeks manipulating digital images, composing their own tracks or re-mixing existing songs into their own creation. They worked with a music animateur, musician, writer, digital artist, and the education department of the Aldeburgh Festival. The work was recorded on a CD, also designed by the group. The next stage was for the Leiston pupils to use the CD as a starting point to carry out the same sort of exercise reflecting their response to the young offenders' experience and work. The final CD was launched with the combined work of Carlford and Leiston.

xi Sculpture

Of all the arts, however classified, sculpture in all its forms is one of the major features across the world, across the centuries, from the Parthenon to the Statue of Liberty, from Africa to Europe. However, numerically by artist and artwork it is one of the smaller and least mentioned arts in schools. Nevertheless, some secondary schools specifically teach sculpture; for instance, Creighton Comprehensive School had five art rooms – of which two were Graphic Studios, two Painting Studios, and the '3D Room, which is for sculpture' (Pottery was separate from Art and in a downstairs workshop.) (Hunter Davies, 1976, p.117). Further, sculpture is specifically noted in the 'Breadth of study' section of Key Stage 3 'Art and Design' in the National Curriculum *Handbook*:

> *During the key stages, pupils should be taught the knowledge, skills and understanding through:*
>
> *(c) using a range of materials and processes, including ICT (for example, painting, collage, print making, digital media, textiles, sculpture)*
>
> (DfEE and QCA, 1999, secondary, p.169)

Arguably sculpture is a more difficult art to teach and learn in a school for practical and skills reasons. Therefore it was one of the arts that suffered from the strengthening of the 'doing' over the 'seeing' in the government's 1977 *Curriculum 11–16* polarity. This stressed that for this age group the study of art 'is essentially, if not wholly, a practical activity' (DES, 1977, p.37). In 'doing-emphatic' periods, when 'appreciating' had been downgraded, sculpture was bound to be barely included.

However, the National Curriculum's final point about Art and Design in Key Stage 3 not only specifically includes sculpture as an example, but under 'Breadth of Study' points out:

> *pupils should be taught the* **knowledge**, **skills and understanding** *through: Investigating art, craft and design in the locality, in a variety of genres, styles and traditions, and from a range of historical, social and cultural contexts (for example in original and reproduction form, during visits to museums, galleries and sites, on the internet).*
>
> (Art and Design, 1999, p.21)

A 'sculpture walk' can be carried out in many areas – taking in modest carvings as well as memorial statues and churches. Homework can be set for each pupil to find, look at, and describe six statues or carvings.

For sculpture to be properly included there has to be full coverage of architecture, of learning to enjoy what you see, and of the range of materials used, including stone, metal, wood, and plastics. Pupils are fascinated by the 'lost wax' process, by which cast-iron sculptures are cast, for instance *The Hare* by Barry Flanagan in the last decade of the last century.

Appreciation can be taught by sharpening the eye, and teaching the concepts for analysis. Technical terms have to be learnt, but sadly this has not always been done. Even schools with modern structures in the grounds have not properly directed the pupils' attention to them. One 1961 London school had a fine piece of aluminium abstract sculpture designed as part of the building, but it was over thirty years before it was given a sign with the name of its sculptor and title: *The Tree of Knowledge*. The point has interestingly been made that:

> There would seem to be an especially important need for a technical vocabulary in respect of architecture and sculpture, for ordinary language is somewhat impoverished in names for shapes and spatial configurations – a factor that may contribute to the difficulty many people appear to find in appreciating the three-dimensional arts other than as regards any representational interest they may have.
>
> (Redfern, 1986, p.19)

We have spoken about architectural difficulties earlier, and re-stress that the 'difficult words', or 'jargon' as they were called by many teachers some years ago, are not so hard (as the polysemous vernacular vocabulary really is). Instead, they give a concept that helps not only language, but perception. The range of work that should be regarded as 'sculpture' is wider than often thought. For instance, an Edinburgh primary school in the 1970s worked with Ken Wolverton to build a dragon in an open space from scrap iron and cement. Brian Dunstone spent two years as 'sculptor in residence' in a Hertfordshire comprehensive at around the same time.

An Ofsted report mentions a visiting sculptor using wood:

> At Castleview Combined School in Slough an annual arts week included visits to the school by a sculptor whose big wood carvings inspired the pupils when they were given the chance to carve large trunks of timber. The art work in this school effectively promotes the pupils' cultural development through the regular use of examples of the work of a variety of artists and through the use of a fine collection of artefacts such as African masks and Indian dolls.
>
> (Jones, 1998, p.13)

We suspect that in many schools sculpture may have been lowered in focus because it smacked of highfalutin', upper-class interest. In fact the teaching of 'sculptural appreciation' (not a frequently used term) can be a way into a range of cultures. Nigeria had some of the finest and most ancient terracotta sculpture in sub-Saharan Africa in the Nok era, and a thousand years later the Yoruba in the south-western part of the country made equally fine sculptures. (Hodge, 1982, p.57) In a different Nigerian tradition brass-casting was used from the twelfth century for a wonderful range of sculptures.

The arts, crafts, humanities, and personal development of the pupils would be advanced by the appropriate incorporation of sculpture into the overall arts curriculum.

xii Textiles

Throughout human history textiles in various forms have been important, ranging from pure decorative art to essentially functional items with virtually no aesthetic aspect. Most have combined function with decoration. Traditionally the term meant a *woven* fabric, from the Latin *texere* meaning 'to weave'. Not very long ago the texture of weaving was evident on so many fabrics, and, indeed, weaving was not only a key British industry but hand-weaving in homes a common artistic hobby. Now a huge range of textiles is factory produced with manufactured fibres, chiefly from petro-chemicals, such as nylon, polyester, and acrylic.

The National Curriculum 'Design and Technology' includes fabrics by such generalised terms as the following from Key Stage 2:

> *Pupils should be taught . . . how the working characteristics affect the way they are used.*
>
> *Pupils should be taught the knowledge, skills and understanding through investigating and evaluating a range of familiar products.*
>
> (DfEE and QCA, 1999, secondary, p.95)

However, specificities of the craft of textiles are not mentioned and there is little or no encouragement to give a proper place for the art of designing textiles. The tradition schools have inherited has been largely 'trade' influenced. 'Needlework' was taught to girls in the middle years of the last century as an occupational training. For instance, at the end of World War II there were in London eight specialist schools for girls in 'the needle trades', with a total of 891 pupils – the largest specialism other than 'Engineering' and 'Building'. The 'trades' included 'dressmaking, ladies tailoring, embroidery, upholstery, millinery, lingerie and corset-making' (LCC, 1947, pp.232–7). The comprehensive schools of the last forty years of the century largely placed textiles in that 'practical' tradition, with the main focus on clothing, called 'fashion', and very little coverage of other aesthetic/artistic manifestations.

The study of costumes across the ages and across cultures is fascinating from the artistic as well as social and technical angles. A brief pictorial survey can be shown by slide and poster ranging from the ancient Egyptian to the Norman invasion of England (and the taking over of Norman dress by the Britons), from the Tudors to nineteenth-century

Americans, showing the visual variety and use of different materials in different styles. A number of schools have a clear inter-cultural approach: a ten-year pupil described warmly how her class had been shown examples of tie-dye, batique and screen printing from India, Aborigine work in Australia, and Africa.

Of course, the modern functional uses of textiles should be included, from clothing to furnishings. However it is artistically incomplete not to include the range of purely decorative uses, such as tapestry, weaving, and 'furnishings' that have major decorative aims.

There is also the historical, inter-cultural appreciation of textile art. Tapestries of the eighteenth century fascinate young people, for instance Peter van den Hecke's *Two Scenes from the Story of Don Quixote*, from 1724. Similarly there are many well preserved rugs which are real works of art, for instance from sixteenth-century Persia.

Textiles were an art form in most parts of the Islamic world from the earliest times. A Yemen tenth-century cotton cloth with applied gilt decoration was a 'benediction' wall-hanging declaring 'Glory is from God'. A spectacular Fatimid treasure of that time was a world map woven of blue silk with each feature identified in gold, silver, or silk writing. Block-printed linen was very widely built into fourteenth-century Islamic art. The largest range of late medieval Islamic textiles are from Egypt; Mamluk really led the Mediterranean market. Even European Renaissance paintings of the Virgin Mary echoed official Arabic design and wording. Indeed, many Mamluk Arabic Islamic textiles were preserved in Western Catholic cathedrals as shrouds for monarchs and as ecclesiastical vestments (Hillenbrand, 1999, p.157).

Closer to home and more recent is the marvellous approach to textiles by the British 'Arts and Crafts' movement, which aimed to re-unite design and craftsmanship, saw craft as a tool in moral reform, and revived regional crafts for a wide range of people. William Morris gave textiles a new life, and the embroidered and painted textiles of the movement are inspiring. His own block-printed designs (for example *Evenlode*, 1883) and silk embroidery panels (for example *Olive and Rose*, 1900) are examples of the kind of embroidery that should be shown for appreciation. Indeed Morris' 1893 article *Textiles* could almost be used as the core of a school's textiles curriculum. For instance, these brief extracts:

> *The noblest of the weaving arts is Tapestry, in which there is nothing mechanical: it may be looked upon as a mosaic of pieces of colour made up of dyed threads, and is capable of producing wall ornaments of any degree of elaboration within the proper limits of duly considered decorative work. . . . Last of the methods of ornamenting cloth comes Embroidery: of the design for which it must be said that one*

of its aims should be the exhibition of beautiful material. Furthermore, it is not worth doing unless it is either very copious and rich, or very delicate – or both. For such an art nothing patchy or scrappy, or half-starved, should be done. . . . Never forget the material you are working with, and try always to use it for what it can do best: if you feel yourself hampered with the material in which you are working, instead of being helped by it, you have so far not learned your business. . . . The special limitations of the material should be a pleasure to you, not a hindrance. It is the pleasure in understanding the capabilities of a special material, and using them for suggesting (not imitating) natural beauty and incident, that gives the raison d'être of decorative art.

(Naylor, 1988, pp.213–17)

Weaving, embroidery, and decorative uses of fabrics from different cultures should be part of the cultural aspect of a school curriculum by museum and art gallery visits, and especially by good quality reproductions and projected slides. Sometimes actual examples can be borrowed and displayed. If at all possible there should be direct 'hands on' experience of weaving and other textile-art approaches, such as embroidery and block printing – even tapestry collages. The pupils' overall arts curriculum needs the contribution of textiles.

xiii Typography and book design

ICT has brought to most users some real sense of typography and page layout – for the first time the choice of typeface, size, and position is rapidly facilitated, albeit usually at a fairly simple level. However, book design and the appreciation of typography is rarely taught. We have grown up with pages of print and rarely consider the art. Still less is whole-book design focused on. Indeed, even the vocabulary is largely omitted: how many pupils have heard 'copy' as a noun for the text to be designed; 'end-paper'; 'gathering'? The National Curriculum uses the terms 'lower- and upper-case letters' (DfEE and QCA , 1999, secondary, p.53), but many teachers still use the term 'small letters' and very rarely is the meaning of 'case' explained. There are references in the Key Stages 3 and 4 'media' section:

Pupils should be taught:

a   how meaning is conveyed in texts that includes print, images and sometimes sounds

b   how choice of form, layout and presentation contribute to effect [for example, font, caption, illustration in printed text, sequencing, framing, soundtrack in moving image text]

(National Curriculum, English, 1999, p.50)

In the 1960s and 70s one of the authors included layout in textbooks for younger secondary schools on both newspapers and advertisements (Marland, 1967, 1974) as part of the 'discriminating reader' approach. However, there still appears to be little of this done.

From the 1930s there was specific teaching of 'book crafts' in 'Senior Schools', and this was regarded as craftwork for *general* education, not a specific occupational training. As one author, then Inspector of Handicraft and Science in Birmingham Education Authority, stressed:

> *They are real crafts, from the first producing articles, which are of recognised utility. . . . As such they afford opportunities for the growth of sound taste and judgement in appraising the technical and artistic qualities of articles in common use in the life of the people.*
>
> (Collins, 1938, p.2)

These courses stressed that they were developing in pupils 'the power of appreciating good design and workmanship'. There was an emphasis on 'the appearance of the article'– size, proportion, binding, and the 'decoration' of the book, including lettering (by hand with pen or brush). Printing was included in many courses, more from a craft point of view than as part of the appreciation of typography.

Although the term or concept 'typography' does not appear in the National Curriculum 'Art and design' document, nor is 'the book' seen as an example of either a craft or technology, we suggest that the whole-school Arts policy should include book design and typography. Photocopied examples of layouts make good exercises, and OHPs of alternative approaches to the same wording of, say a title page, lead to a good discussion in a lesson. The design of current books can be compared and key points highlighted. Even hand-bound and specifically decorated books can be considered. Antiquarian books surprise and fascinate many pupils, and a display is stimulating.

xiv Visual arts

In a visually dominant world, visual literacy is becoming as critical to young people's body of skills and perceptions as the literacy of reading and writing. We need to have knowledge of and to be able to interpret what we see, be it a painting, sculpture, photograph, or film image. What is seen within the screen or the frame helps to determine one's perception of what is beyond the screen and the frame.

We can read visual images more quickly than ever. Look at the 'shorthand' in many of the commercial breaks on television. Many television programmes, especially those for young people, switch from one image or item to another and use multi-images.

This elementary form of visual literacy needs to be deepened and enhanced by a greater contemplation of what is seen. It requires both direct contact with works of art and practical creative experience. This can help to develop such life skills as observation, the ability to interpret, imagination, self-awareness, and a flexibility of thought and action.

For example, the four principles underpinning the education work at the Royal Academy of Arts are:

- works of art can inspire creative and aesthetic pleasure and impart knowledge of a wide range of intellectual disciplines;
- there is no substitute for the original work of art;
- learning from a work of art depends on visual literacy;
- first-hand experience of the creative process is essential for developing the whole individual.

This is not to diminish the value of the excellent websites and CD-ROMs offered by galleries and museums here and abroad. They provide introductions to and insights into the works of art, as well as vital historical, cultural and aesthetic background. But the aim should be, wherever and whenever possible, to lead on from second-hand to first-hand experience.

The visual arts, perhaps more than any other art form, can permeate a school – its curriculum and environment. Examples might be a series of exhibitions of artworks relating to specific themes from the various subject areas (not just art and design) that are accessible to all members of the school rather than tucked away in a classroom. Such exhibitions should, of course, include pupils' and teachers' own work.

In addition, every school can readily build a two-way relationship with a local, regional or national gallery or museum, with the involvement of practising artists working with teachers and pupils. An artist might be prepared to set up a studio in the school on a long-term basis. Some galleries and museums, such as the one at Reading, have established loan schemes whereby schools can exhibit a range of artefacts from the museum or gallery's permanent collection.

This kind of scheme has its origins in the innovative loan schemes initiated and run by several enlightened local authorities, such as Cheshire, Hertfordshire, Inner London, and Leicestershire, in the fifties and sixties. These, for example, put Henry Moore and Barbara Hepworth sculptures on to school premises. Which school will be first with an artwork by Damien Hirst or Rachel Whiteread?

Today, such initiatives have even greater potential for two broad reasons. They are able to promote and reflect the diverse cultural traditions and innovations that local communities and their schools now embrace. Second, they can be inter-related with other subjects.

The education department of the Royal Academy of Arts makes relevant connections between its exhibitions and the study of such subjects as geography, history, religious education, music, textiles, media studies, psychology, sociology, ICT, design and technology, and, of course, art. It does this with such diverse exhibitions as Frank Auerbach, Rembrandt, and early Ukiyo-e treasures of Japan.

Finally, a school's own approach to the visual arts should always seek to broaden the horizons and challenge the perceptions of its pupils – and indeed of its teachers. No other art form can do so more immediately and consistently. The aim should be constantly to hear the comment: 'I see what you mean.'

xv Wood and metalwork

The very terms 'wood and metalwork' have a really old-fashioned ring about them! The 1937 Board of Education's *Handbook of Suggestions* for 'Public Elementary Schools' recommended these as 'rightly the crafts most universally taught boys in Elementary schools', especially as 'the materials employed . . . offer just enough resistance to cutting and shaping to make suitable demands on the muscular control of boys of this age' – an interesting curriculum inclusion criteria (Board of Education, 1937, pp.262–3). Although the text praises 'the range of beautiful objects that can be made', it mainly emphasises the 'degree of accuracy necessary in working the material employed', as 'an error of 1/16th of an inch in a woodwork joint, or of 1/100th of an inch in metalwork fitting, results in a misfit which is easily perceived by the pupil responsible'.

Despite the overwhelming practicality of the aims there was also a focus on design, for instance in woodwork considering 'the particular proportions of a rectangle . . . or the particular sweep of a curve'; the 'arrangement of colour and tone and the modification of outline should be considered in relation to the particular wood used'. The Board rightly stressed that 'in this way the boys will gradually develop their own standards in Design'. Art is almost implicit, as 'work which is inspired by ideas such as these may quite fairly be described as creative' (Board of Education, 1937, p.265).

In most courses there was a combination of 'prevocational training' with the idea 'that the dull child should not be entirely unable to use his hands should ill luck fall his way'. This led to 'the rather low status of the crafts subjects' (Eggleston, 1971, p.176). Yet from the 1930s onward there was also a strong arts element in these courses. The teachers going into the 'Technical Block' to teach 'Handicrafts' were trained in an ethos of making pupils sensitive to materials, structures, forms, and surfaces. Indeed a William Morris philosophy, combining the arts and crafts, lay within the courses. As one teacher later put it: 'If you can make a good joint you will be able to write good poetry.'

The Arts and Crafts principles deepened and sensitised the quasi-vocational approach: these were traditional arts, and the Morris legacy was that they should bring together 'design unity, joy in labour, individualism, and regionalism' (Cumming and Kaplan, 1991, p.7). The movement had a 'strict design morality'. Pugin's famous aphorism was a deeply artistic point: beauty depended on 'the fitness of the design to the purpose for which it was intended'. Ruskin demanded design which used form, scale, and materials to express 'men's delight in God's work', and the nineteenth-century tradition of craft techniques from the Arts and Crafts movement underlay many school 'handicraft' courses. The reuniting of 'Arts and Crafts' from Ruskin and Morris was alive in many a 'manual training school' or 'Handicraft suite' of mid-twentieth-century secondary schools: grammar, technical, and secondary modern.

The Arts and Crafts movement brought together the concepts of 'art' and 'craft', workers in different specialisms, and very significantly enabled one person to work across what might seem to some as separate skills. For instance, one man described by himself and others as 'an artist' was 'working in stained glass, wood and metal church decoration'. Thus, for instance, the Guild of Handicraft inaugurated in Toynbee Hall in 1888 was devoted to the disciplines of 'practical work: woodwork, metal work and decorative painting'. It certainly deserves a unit of study, as the Century Guild put it, on 'the Unity of all the Aesthetic Arts' (Cumming and Kaplan, 1991, p.25). The unit should bring out the relationship between architecture and furniture, glass, painting, textiles, metalwork, and jewellery. Indeed the Guild was founded 'to render all branches the sphere no longer of the tradesman, but of the artist' and to integrate building, decoration, glass painting, pottery, woodcarving and metalwork' to their rightful place besides painting and sculpture'. Typography and book design were also seen as harmonious, as was writing.

Of course, the Arts and Crafts movement had its roots in late nineteenth-century Britain, but 'these principles were adopted in America and to a lesser extent in Continental Europe' (Cumming and Kaplan, 1991, p.6). Its traditions have not fully dominated all wood and metalwork in this country since, but it has been very strong, especially in its emphasis not on adopting a definite style, but a trueness to materials, function, and workmanship – seeking sweetness, beauty, and practicality. Eric Gill looked back in his *Autobiography* at what he saw as the bringing together of practical endeavour and idealism, hoping that he had 'done something towards re-integrating bed and board, the small farm and workshop, the home and the school, earth and heaven' (Gill, 1940, p.282). Thus related, and connected to English vernacular architecture and classical architecture, there is a strong British cultural tradition, and this should be demonstrated. For instance, William Morris' 1889 'Red House' in Upton, Kent has wood and metal work of British tradition and craftsmanship and has been an inspiration to schools.

The intercultural aspects of woodwork and metalwork need stressing, but have not apparently often featured in school courses. An important example is Islamic design in Africa. As one specialist review put it: 'Craft specializations and aesthetic sensibilities closely followed the spread of the faith in East and West Africa, across the Sahara, spreading throughout the Sahel and encroaching upon the forest zone' (Bravemann, 1983, p.7). A marvellous Swahili large, high back, ebony chair with arms and footrest would be an interesting and impressive example to show on a slide to a class. Similarly, a modern version of a traditional Koran stand: 'Two flat boards hinged in the centre with upper surfaces deeply incised with triangles, squares, and circles.' There are apparently not many major examples of woodwork in Islamic buildings, though a few of great interest, for instance:

- The sarcophagus of sandalwood and ivory for Shah Ismail 1, in 1524, in Ardabil in Persia (p.235).
- A wooden cover (inlaid in ivory) for an oblong copy of the Qur'an, in Egypt from the tenth century (p.57).

And in metal:

- Bronze and iron brazier from c.750, cast by the lost-wax method, with two griffins with outstretched wings, in Egypt (p.18).
- Silver-gilt dish, ninth-century Iran (p.48).

- Bronze plate inlaid with 7-colour cloisonné enamel, showing Alexander the Great ascending to heaven, twelfth century, Byzantine and Islamic (p.155).

- Brass hexagonal table, inlaid with silver dated 1328, Cairo, with the words 'Glory to our Lord the Sultan, al-Malik al-Nasim Muhammad' repeated 54 times (p.154).

(Hillenbrand, 1999, page references as noted)

All such examples are best shown by projected slides, though there are a few museums in the UK with examples of Islamic wood or metal work.

Finally, it is amazing how examples very close to hand and eye are not seen and used. How many pupils are shown examples of Tudor woodwork, fire irons, or grates? The eighteenth-century classical revival in Britain went to Rome for its architectural style (as discussed in this section under Architecture) and the railings of the basements and steps to the front doors of those houses and neighbouring squares are reproductions in cast iron of Roman spears and funeral urns. Intercultural memories are literally on our doorsteps.

Ideally designing, making, and appreciating the work of others should be for all. Primary schools can do very little wrought ironwork, but metal can be handled and studied. Some wood-working is possible on a small scale, and has a deep and lasting effect on the pupils. The National Curriculum for Key Stage 2 includes 'knowledge and understanding of materials'. 'Breadth of Study' includes 'investigating and evaluating a range of familiar products', and 'working with tools' to 'measure, mark out, cut and shape a range of materials'. It would be good if this could include wood more often and even metal sometimes.

In the secondary school the 'workbench' dominates – thus there is plenty of 'making' in wood, but this means that the study is too limited in scale, affordable material, and style for a truly comprehensive course. MDF dominates too often. Most workshops have virtually no displays of artefacts, in reality or picture, and there is little true training of observation. Metalwork is less common, though there is some good wrought-iron work and even some cast-iron.

In neither material is there much reference to individual designer-craftspeople or biographical support for the crafts. Visual Arts, Music, and Drama teachers include artists, but wood and metalwork artists are often omitted. How many pupils are shown pictures of the woodwork of Gordon Russell, Chippendale, Ambrose Heal, Ernest Gimpson, or Viscount Linley? Iron workers are even less known. How many have been told about the metalwork of Ioujou, who did the gates at Hampton Court? One 'anthology of iron', *Decorative Ironwork*, shows photographs of iron screens from cathedrals all over Europe. It gives examples of the displays of pictures or programmes of slides that students should be shown (Zimelli and Vergio, 1966).

Although there is a fair quantity and range of woodwork in most environments, very many young people have not been taught how 'to read' woodwork. They have not had different woods contrasted, studied the grain, or thought about joints. The purpose of panelling, in which the grain of the wood is being controlled by the different sections working against each other, has not been explained.

It could be said that just as a school has 'anthologies' of poetry in the library and of performed music on CD, there should be anthologies of materials and forms, such as stone, brick, wood, and metal. For every school to have a full collection would be difficult or impossible. However, much can be achieved by modest, specially commissioned, permanent but moveable displays. For instance, one school had two hanging boards, each about a metre square, which beautifully displayed the key wood joints in a way which was both very clear and aesthetically pleasing. Similarly schools have had wall displays of wrought iron, demonstrating its practicality, variety, and decorativeness. Larger items can also be displayed, for instance pieces of timber and modern 'reconstructed' timber.

There were times when Local Authorities toured displays – for instance, the old London County Council toured superb design displays for school public spaces, including all the crafts. This is the kind of thing schools cannot normally do alone, and the country needs to consider touring metalwork and woodwork displays for schools. The Crafts Council Photostore slide-hire service and Colour Printout service (address in Appendix 2) is a good way of bringing in visual representation, and there is a wood, though not a metal, section.

On the continuum between the extreme of 'pure craft' and 'pure art', both wood and metalwork occupy a significant and large spread, with examples at both ends. The school's overall planning should ensure that the artistic dimension and inter-cultural interest should be part of the pupils' imaginative experience.

xvi Conclusion

The range of the arts for creating and appreciating should be as wide as possible, even if some are only occasionally and briefly included. In this section we have chosen the division of 'the art forms' to facilitate school curriculum planning, but of course we realise that aesthetic and technical divisions could be different in many ways. We also fully accept that other art forms could have been included, for instance: stained glass, jewellery, and furniture. Their omission is not an indication of their level of value and importance within a school's coverage of the arts. The distinction between 'art' and 'craft' is obviously a difficult one, but we urge the continuity of aesthetic consideration well across the whole range.

3 PLANNING ACROSS THE SCHOOL

Pressures in schools and the shortage of planning time can make whole-school review of an aspect very difficult. Often both primary and secondary schools find themselves considering one art at a time, reviewing it, and adjusting the planning of the delivery. We strongly recommend a whole-school arts review and a whole-school overview plan in relation to all the curriculum aims. Specific ideas from specialists in the school or advice from outside would of course be incorporated.

The overall arts policy should not merely be an aggregate of the description of the separate policies for each of the arts. There must be a creative interaction between over-arching whole-school visions of pupil growth and input from the focus of each art. Thus the whole-school arts education policy contributes to wider aspects of the overall curriculum plan. Conversely, the closely focused arts aspects are enriched by the wider support and input. For example, the mathematics teacher's highlighting of geometry's contribution to aesthetics and the historian's inclusion of the place of the arts in the life of an earlier society, are part of the arts curriculum. Conversely, specific arts teaching contributes towards personal and social growth as well as towards literacy and inter-cultural understanding.

3.1 Auditing the school's arts provision

In 1998, the Royal Society of Arts (RSA), in association with the Harbourside Centre in Bristol, carried out a pilot project to see how an arts audit might be a starting point for schools to improve standards of arts provision. Six schools took part in the project, which was supported by Crayola, South West Arts, the Arts Council of England (ACE), and the Department for Culture, Media and Sport (DCMS). Its successful outcomes meant that the audit process was repeated in other areas of the country.

The RSA issued a detailed guide on auditing (see *Investing in the Arts: How to carry out a school arts audit and compile an arts statement*, RSA, 1998). A revised version has been included in the Artsmark application pack to help schools take part in this exciting new scheme run by ACE. A large number of schools have, by now, carried out this audit exercise. It enables them to assess strengths and weaknesses, to identify opportunities for improvement and innovation, and to estimate the resources required to take advantage of those opportunities.

Schools report that they find it rewarding not just in terms of gathering information about their arts provision, but also as a way to create interest in and understanding of the arts across the school. They use it as a basis for forming new partnerships within the school and with galleries and museums, performing companies and ensembles, and individual artists. The audit can also be used to prepare for an Ofsted inspection, and to follow the DfES guidance on the contents of school prospectuses (see below).

Here is what some schools have said about doing an audit.

> *The most valuable part was having time to discuss needs and initiatives with colleagues from our own and from other schools. It is always a boost to meet people with similar enthusiasms.*

> *It made us realise how much of the arts we cover and how we give a high priority to teaching the arts.*

> *It enabled us to gain a whole school view of our arts provision and has been useful in helping us to prepare for our arts college bid.*

▰ What an audit can tell you

The benefits most frequently cited by schools are that doing an audit:

- gives a clearer picture of arts provision;
- enhances the profile of the arts within and beyond the school;
- improves staff liaison within and across subject areas;
- identifies opportunities for teachers' professional development; and
- creates new relationships between teachers, governors and parents, and with artists and arts organisations beyond the school.

In the circulars on the contents of school prospectuses (7/98 and 8/98, July 1998), the DfEE suggested that schools include a clear statement on arts policy and provision, which includes, where appropriate, plans for improving facilities. It also recommended providing a range of cultural experiences and opportunities including:

- visits (for example to art galleries, concerts, theatres and crafts facilities);
- collaborative opportunities for participation in the arts (for example with other educational institutions, arts organisations and local groups);
- links with arts specialists and practitioners (for example through theatre in education, artists in residence, local organisations' education programmes);
- time given to arts experiences and practice in and outside the formal curriculum;
- arts qualifications or expertise of staff, including any commitments to improve quality of arts teaching, for example through further staff training, secondments, and so on.

An audit can readily provide this kind of 'nuts and bolts' information. The areas covered would include:

Content
- the extent and type of art forms provided;
- the balance between different art forms and cultures;
- how far the arts are used in other subject areas.

Resources
- the equipment, facilities and dedicated spaces for each art form;
- the extent to which arts subjects use the school's ICT facilities;
- the expertise of those staff who teach an arts subject;
- the artistic skills of other staff members, governors and parents.

Pupils
- whether all pupils have direct experience of a range of art forms;
- the quantity, quality and diversity of arts experiences gained by different groups of pupils at each key stage;
- how well the school ensures equal opportunity for its pupils to enjoy each art form and for access to facilities and resources;

- how much time pupils spend on arts activities in addition to the core curriculum;
- the level of pupils' involvement with arts activities out of school hours;
- whether there are regular displays of pupils' work and opportunities for them to perform.

Key skills
- the extent to which the arts are used in teaching literacy and numeracy, and other subjects, through cross-curricular activities;
- the school's awareness of the potential, and its readiness, to teach key skills through the arts.

Planning
- what targets to set for improving standards, increasing and enhancing provision;
- how to begin planning to fill gaps in provision highlighted by the audit.

The process for an arts audit can therefore provide:
- a structure for schools to assess, and regularly revisit, the work they are doing in the arts;
- a means for teachers to judge what are arts experiences of quality and whether they are providing them; and
- a focus and stimulus for managers towards future action through the school development plan and for target-setting.

Getting started

The secret of doing a successful audit is good management. It takes a little time and might involve some minor expense, such as a day's cover for a teacher. But most schools find they can readily fit it into the everyday organisational and curriculum schedule by agreeing a realistic timetable for doing the audit. Overall, the benefits far outweigh any resource spent.

The first step is to write down some specific outcomes that your school wants to achieve by doing the audit. This will:

- give your audit a clear focus;
- enable your school to get maximum benefit from the work involved;

- better inform the arts statement; and
- help in planning for the future.

Second, discuss the idea of the audit, and what it involves at a staff meeting; with all those staff who teach the arts, or have an interest in them; with the governors; and with the parents' association or PTA.

Explain why you want to do the audit and its likely benefits for the school. Your aim should be to build broad support for the audit and a commitment to use the results to improve provision. If the school has an artist in residence, or a good working relationship with a local or regional arts organisation or company, encourage them to take an interest in, advise on, or be involved with the audit.

The size of the school determines how far all the staff (teaching and non-teaching) can be involved. But it is important to consult and work with every head of a subject faculty or department or subject co-ordinator (not just those with a responsibility for the arts), individually or through the school management team. The next step is to form your audit team.

Appoint a team

Gather together a small team of 'auditors' – for example, a teacher, governor and parent. Ask for volunteers, or invite people with particular interest or expertise in the arts. Some schools involve an artist or arts administrator, and a pupil as well. The aim is to give all those with a stake in the school a sense of ownership for the audit. Try to ensure that every group (staff, governors, parents, pupils) is kept informed of progress, and asked to comment on proposed targets for improvement.

Agree arrangements

Arrange a meeting of the audit team to agree:

- aims, objectives, ways of working, and desired outcomes;
- a timetable (including regular review meetings);
- the information to be collected, who holds it and/or where it is held;
- the people to interview or consult about arts provision and resources;
- an estimate of the amount of money, staff time and other resources to be allocated to carrying out the audit.

Decide what to ask

Devise a series of questions about the information you need. Make them as straightforward as possible (see Checklist). Find out too about people's attitudes to and perceptions of the arts and their place in the curriculum.

Publicise the audit

Create a buzz in the school about the audit being carried out:

- post notices on boards and websites (perhaps devised and designed by pupils);
- organise special displays of pupils' performance and art work;
- encourage everyone to come to you with information and ideas.

Doing an audit usually sparks lively discussion about the school's arts provision. Earmark time to talk informally with interested colleagues, governors, parents and pupils about the school and the arts. Sparking pupils' enthusiasm can be a valuable way to involve those teachers who feel they have no direct concern for the arts.

The cost of an audit

An arts audit costs very little, if any, money to carry out – especially for a small school. For large schools, the main financial costs can be paying for one or two days' supply cover for the teacher(s) compiling the audit, any additional clerical help, and publishing the results. However, you can reduce the expense by:

- timetabling the work to avoid the need for cover;
- linking the work to preparing for an Ofsted inspection, compiling or updating the school development plan, setting targets, or preparing the school prospectus;
- incorporating material on the audit within existing documents, such as the school development plan, prospectus or governors' annual report. Where a school needs extra resources, the process of auditing provision and developing targets to raise standards could be eligible for grants through the Standards Fund and allocated to schools by the local education authority (see DfES guidance: LEA/054/2001 (*The Standards Fund 2002-03*). Talk to your LEA about it.

How much time you need to compile the audit will vary according to the size of the school. It usually takes between two and four days' work, often spread over two to four weeks. The time involved can be reduced by linking it to other school tasks.

Carrying out the audit

Compile a calendar

Compile an arts calendar of all events and activities involving the school and its pupils, in the curriculum, outside school, with local community groups or other schools.

Collect the evidence

Bring together all the written material showing how far the school's thinking, policy and practice include the arts. Formal documents should include: school timetable and extra-curricular activities, school development plan, staff development and INSET plan, departmental action plans and policy statements, current set of targets for improvement, Ofsted report, school prospectus and governors' annual report, any LEA guidelines on the arts and the school's response to them, and minutes of staff and governors' meetings referring to the arts. Informal material might include: local press cuttings, photographs of arts activities such as displays and performances by pupils or work with artists in residence, and school newsletters.

List the resources

Identify the equipment and other physical resources available to the arts both in school and outside, for example run by community or commercial agencies, arts organisations, and other schools. Be realistic: your life is busy enough, so do not count every paint pot or crayon. It is better to list levels of availability or sourcing of materials (for example generous, readily available, adequate or inadequate).

Spread the load

A useful way to make the audit more manageable is to treat it as a series of mini-audits – of staffing, pupil involvement in the arts, funding, accommodation, use of information and communication technology (ICT) in the arts, cross-curricular links with other subjects, external support sources, and so on.

The Checklist suggests areas you might want to investigate and what quantitative and qualitative information to collect. Choose the areas most relevant to your school.

Checklist of areas to cover in the audit

The curriculum
- Which arts subjects are taught at each Key Stage?
- How far is the school curriculum regarded by arts staff as balanced and broadly based?
- How far are the new technologies used in the arts curriculum?
- How well does the curriculum provide pupils with knowledge and understanding of, and participation in, the arts of different cultures?

Staffing
- What is the level of staffing for the arts – permanent, peripatetic, part-time and voluntary?
- What qualifications and additional artistic skills and talents do staff have?
- What are the training needs of staff involved in the arts?
- What artistic skills and talents do governors and parents have which the school can use to enhance provision and support the formal staff?

Professional development
- How many teachers have taken part in arts-related INSET this year?
- What courses have they been on?
- How has this affected practice?
- How is their new expertise passed on to colleagues?

Inspection
- What does the latest Ofsted inspection report say about the arts in your school?
- Have any aspects of arts provision needing attention been addressed?

Funding
- What funding is available for each art form offered by the school?
- What additional funding sources are available to support arts activities beyond the school's own budget?
- What costs do parents and/or pupils incur for taking part in school-generated arts activities?

Auditing the school's arts provision

Accommodation
- Which areas or facilities in the school are specifically or exclusively used for arts?
- What other spaces are used by each art form?
- What is their fitness for purpose and availability?
- What gaps exist in suitable accommodation for the arts?
- What facilities outside the school are used for timetabled or extra-curricular arts activities?

The local authority
- Does your LEA send out any guidelines on the arts?
- What advice or support services does it offer?
- Does any local authority department arrange arts events or opportunities for pupils?
- How far does the school take advantage of such services?

Other external support
- How much support comes from collaborations with other agencies, for example arts organisations?
- How often does the school work with artists on curriculum, extra-curricular and out-of-school activities or events?
- What collaborative activities are there with other schools?
- How many, and what type of, arts visits are made by which pupils through the school?

Pupils' involvement in the arts
What proportion of pupils at each Key Stage:
- take which arts subjects for what length of time;
- are involved in extra-curricular arts activities;
- receive instrumental music lessons;
- have the opportunity to work with artists or arts groups in residence or at arts venues;
- go on school visits to arts venues;
- sit GCSE, A-level or GNVQ/NVQ exams, or other specialist qualifications in arts subjects, and what grades are achieved?

Assessment procedures
- How do you report to parents about their child's achievements in the arts?

- How do you keep a record of their progress?
- What criteria do you use to assess their progress?
- At what times of the year do you carry out assessments?

Transfer between schools
- What information is passed on to colleagues?
- What information is passed on to a child's next school?
- What information is received from a child's previous school?

Equal opportunities
- What arts provision is available to children with special needs?
- Does it differ from that offered to other pupils?
- Are special arrangements or equipment available to ensure equal access?
- Are arts activities equally accessible to girls and boys?

Involving governors
- How do you report to governors about the arts?
- Which governors are involved in the arts in school?
- What activities are they involved in?

Involving parents
- How do you tell parents about arts activities?
- Do you organise arts activities involving parents?

Working with other schools
- When do you meet with other schools for arts events or activities?
- What activities have been carried out together?

Community involvement
- Do your pupils put on performances outside the school?
- Do local community groups use the school's arts facilities?
- Do you organise arts activities involving the local community, as groups or individuals?

Publicity
- How often does the local media (press, radio, television) report on your arts activities?

- Do you keep a photographic record of arts events, displays and activities at your school?
- Do you keep programmes of concerts, plays and other events?

Knowing what people think

An important part of the audit is to find out the views of the teachers, governors, parents and pupils about arts provision and the opportunities for improvement.

Ask the staff:
- what they do in the arts and how they do it;
- what they consider to be doing well;
- what could be done better – and what is needed to do so.

Ask governors, parents and pupils:
- the three best things about the school's arts provision;
- the three worst things about the school's arts provision;
- what improvements they would like to see.

Publicise the findings

Everyone involved or interested in the audit will want to know what you have found out. Think about who will be interested in your findings inside the school – staff, governors, parents; and outside – other schools, the LEA, parents of prospective pupils, local media, local businesses, potential sponsors of and partners in arts activities. Focus on the main points: 'what we do well', 'where we could do better' and 'how we intend to give pupils a better arts experience'.

Decide on the most appropriate way to get the audit findings across to each group – and remember that reporting on your audit can be a valuable way to create greater interest and activity in the arts, and to encourage people to work and lobby for even better provision. Publicise the findings in attractive, accessible, positive and inexpensive ways. For example:

- publish a short report with examples of pupils' work and photographs of performances;
- set up a display in the school highlighting the main findings, again using photographs and pupils' work; or

- hold a special arts event or festival with visiting artists to bring together and enthuse everyone involved with the school.

You may also want to present the audit findings and the arts statement together as a single document.

▰ Write the Arts Statement

Key questions

Use the findings from your audit to consider three key questions for writing, or rewriting, the school's arts statement:

- What do you want to happen with arts provision?
- How can you make it happen?
- What is needed to make it happen?

Key contents

The statement can contain whatever best meets the needs and aims of the school in relation to the arts. For example, it might list:

- key points from the audit;
- the school's policy on the arts, plus its organisational and curriculum structure for carrying through the policy;
- a guarantee of what the school will provide for every pupil in terms of an arts experience;
- a commitment to work with artists within and beyond the school;
- the expected benefits from having artists work with the school;
- targets to improve arts provision in the future;
- how the school intends to meet those targets.

▰ Use the audit to improve provision

Having completed the audit, you can now assess how to improve or enhance arts provision. The next step is to set priorities for action to meet the targets you have identified in the arts statement, in terms of resources, curriculum development, school organisation, activities, and expertise. Decide which improvements can be done relatively easily or quickly, and which need time, resources, or negotiation to carry through. The audit will have given you some valuable tools to help you do this. For example:

Set benchmarks

Identify benchmarks to refer to as improvements are made. Make sure everyone knows when a target is reached. This builds confidence and keeps the arts in the limelight.

Build networks

Use the audit results and the arts statement as a focus to build networks with other schools and arts organisations, and meet arts teachers and artists.

Plan arts activities

Devise aims and objectives for a programme of work with local, regional and national artists and arts organisations that suit the needs of the school.

Exchange information

Put a report of the audit – and the special features of the school's arts provision – on the Internet. Exchange information and ideas on making particular improvements and share achievements with neighbouring schools – and across the world.

3.2 Pupils as creators, performers, and audience

One of the most difficult tensions in planning the arts curriculum is that between 'audience' and 'participants'. The equilibrium between the two positions changes from time to time, but we should not let the balance swing too far one way. Are we primarily producing participants or audiences? The question is wrongly put: we should be doing both, for the one helps the other. However, a huge majority of our pupils will in the end be audiences of one sort or another. It is not right to criticise this as being passive. Jacob Bronowski put it well:

> *In the moment of appreciation we live again the moment when the creator saw and held the hidden likeness ... We re-enact the creative act, and we ourselves make the discovery again.*
>
> (Bronowski, 1964, p.30)

Some people seem to be still reacting against what was regarded as a form of non-participatory art education of the past. Few schools now spend much time looking at pictures. You can go through the DT departments of most schools and not see a single piece by an artist-craftsman on display, despite the fact that the head of DT says: 'Of course we are teaching children to be designers and respect materials'. It is as if we are frightened of showing them work by other artist-craftsmen. The Calouste Gulbenkian Foundation study in 1980 reported 'primary schools have limited contact with dance outside the school . . . The pupils are unlikely to have experienced any performance by a visiting dance group, any school dance display, day of dance, or performance during the year' (Calouste Gulbenkian, 1980, p.44).

There has been some increase but not much. In the secondary survey, it reported that 'Responses showing visits and displays during the years were so small as to be statistically insignificant, thus confirming the same deficiency noted at primary level' (Calouste Gulbenkian, 1980, p.55). In most schools, pupils are so busy doing that they do very little watching. I am not arguing that we should throw the baby out with the bathwater – we must keep a balance. Keith Swanwick, Professor of Music Education at the London Institute of Education, said: 'Effective teaching in the arts will require us to have children form, perform, and be in audience, if possible with some direct relationship between those activities' (Swanwick, 1983, p.21). The poet George MacBeth got the complementary balance right when he wrote about poetry in 1984:

> I don't believe that writing poetry is more important than reading it. I believe that the two are part of the same process: the imaginative penetration of the world about us. Those who play the verse piano a little themselves will always admire the great virtuosi.

> (MacBeth, 1984, p.185)

The American composer Aaron Copland stresses:

> Listening is its own reward. There are no prizes to be won, no contests of creative listening. But I hold that person fortunate who has the gift, for there are few pleasures in art greater than the secure sense that one can recognise beauty when one comes upon it.

> (Copland, 1952, pp.8–9)

Participating is necessary, both as preparation for being an artist and appreciating. It is vital though that a wide range of 'audience' opportunities are arranged. Why is it that there has always been a major emphasis on reading literature, but not 'reading' architecture, pictures, dance, moving pictures, and drama?

Theatrical or personal?

Across many schools there is a tension between the theatrical and the informal in the performing arts. Most people like the sense of occasion associated with 'going out', and yet we also feel we should be producing informal settings for children. Actually, both are necessary. We need to have visits out and we need to have informal, what could be called 'chamber', performances. There is something very powerful about a full performance, but the same can be true of much simpler presentations. For instance, a dance with a piano accompaniment in a small hall, can be very effective. Being in the same 'chamber' as the performers, without the full performance, scenery, and audience, focuses the mind dramatically.

Visiting an art gallery or theatre is an important experience and ways of democratising it should be sought, but an arts education policy must feature the devising and presenting of performing arts experiences in a range of non-theatrical and often unconventional local settings. This can serve youth, school, and community groups and indeed, give performances a fresh impact. Further, these should not always be cut-down versions of works requiring full performances, but often should be specially devised for the venue and kind of occasion.

Pupils as audiences

We have created an exaggerated split between creating and spectating, which is seen too often as 'merely passive'. Schools should not forget the skill of being a member of an audience. To quote Aaron Copland again: 'Listening is a talent unlike any other talent or gift we possess. We possess it in varying degrees.' There is amongst music lovers a marked tendency to underestimate it. He said: 'Recognising the beautiful in an abstract art like music partakes somewhat of a minor miracle, each time it happens I remain slightly incredulous' (Copland, 1952, pp.8–9). We have underplayed the audience aspect, which is a crucial ingredient for the whole-school life.

These complementary aspects lead to a very wide range of activities:

- both didactic and experiential teaching;
- special events devised to embody the arts;
- opportunities for listening and watching;
- opportunities outside of the course timetable;
- displays;

- local artists, different ethnic groups, and different religious communities;
- a range of audiences for pupils;
- a variety of specially prepared performances by pupils;
- reflection of the arts in the school environment;
- opportunities to encourage the development of skills for the visual arts.

Even music education, moving to improvisation and away from 'great works', has arguably closed its doors to pupils' listening to the music of other cultures. We have undervalued the third side of what Benjamin Britten called 'this holy triangle of composer, performer, and listener' (Britten, 1964, p.20). The Western stress on 'doing' can keep other cultures at bay because it reduces opportunities for pupils to experience unfamiliar musical forms. Although the workshop approach can be used to extend and lead into other cultures, an over-emphasis on creation and performance can detract from responding in one's mind, imagination, and feelings. In our anxiety that art should be 'accessible' we must take care not to restrict the range of arts. The building of a music curriculum out of the creativity of pupils is excellent but not sufficient: our pupils have a *right* to access the music of the cultures of the world.

In *The National Curriculum Handbook for Secondary Teachers*, the drama list of 'knowledge, skills, and understanding' displays a good balance:

> *The range should include:*
>
> a *improvisation and working in role*
> b *devising, scripting and performing in plays*
> c *discussing and reviewing their own and others' performances.*
>
> (DfEE and QCA, 1999, secondary, p.48)

It is important that there is a rich complementary mixture. As Heinz Quilitzsch put it:

> *The task of the artist is not fulfilled simply in the creation of a work, for it only receives its true value through the effect on the observer.*

3.3 Whole-school curriculum planning for the arts

There has to be a whole-school description of the overall arts curriculum before the planning of the delivery is possible. Most secondary schools consider which 'courses' to use to deliver the curriculum and some have unusual divisions in Key Stage 3 at least. Yet most 'curriculum planning' takes the list of National Curriculum 'subjects', debates the time element for each, agonises over the pupil-grouping issues, and leaves it to the 'Subject Department' to plan the curriculum for that subject. Usually this adds to the National Curriculum 'Programme of Study' some aspects of 'cross-curriculum themes' and of the school's aims and philosophy. Since 2001, ideas from the modern version of 'Language Across the Curriculum' would be included, along with the QCA's 'Language at Work in Lessons' (QCA, 2001).

This 'subject by subject' planning does not well suit the arts. Some powerful interconnected themes can be missed along with significant relationships to other aspects of the curriculum. The National Curriculum legislation, as analysed in Chapter 1, Section 3, unintentionally appeared to suggest the separation of 'art' and 'music' as 'subjects', and 'drama' and 'dance' as *part* of the 'subjects' of 'English' and 'Physical Education'. In the June 1988 House of Lords debate on the draft Bill there was a proposal to use only the broad term 'the arts'. Lord Young of Dartington (Michael Young) argued:

> *The point of the arts is that they should be all-embracing or at any rate should cover a very large range and not even stop at what are conventionally thought of as the arts but should merge with crafts and design. The distinction between arts and crafts is a very arbitrary one which very few people devoted to the arts wish to make.*
>
> (Young, 1988, p.723)

Earlier sections have argued the need for starting with an overview of the arts related to the school's over-arching philosophical statement of its aims. The logical next step is to consider the various modes by which that content of attitudes, concepts, skills, and knowledge should be delivered, which in turn needs to incorporate other aspects of the whole-school curriculum that could well be supported by delivery through arts-focused lessons and activities.

The fundamental need is for whole-school planning of the curriculum initially without reference to courses. Arts should be considered as Literacy is. This overview should be as broad as suggested in Chapter 2. Its organising design needs to be shaped round 'art forms', provided it is fully embedded in the detail that different cultures and periods need to be articulated. Whilst most of the actual teaching will be by art form, sometimes there will be a culture focus, sometimes a period one, and sometimes a technological one. For instance, the Japanese Noh play relates to the art form of drama, the stylised approach to medieval form, and Japanese history. The overall planning should firmly put the question 'how?' to one side. That comes next.

Specific and contextual

There is a deep underlying conceptual distinction related to curriculum planning. In considering where we locate aspects of the arts, we should bear in mind a key curriculum-planning aspect: a skill, concept, topic, or fact can be taught either 'specifically' or 'contextually'. This is one of the fundamental concepts of curriculum planning, yet it is rarely focused on, except, for instance, in the QCA's approach to 'literacy across the curriculum' and similarly ICT.

We need to carefully consider the two delivery modes. The first we call the **specific**: for example, 'We are now going to learn about walls'. Mathematics is substantially 'specific', with the context (for example actual statistics, examples of the use of polygons, surveys) brought in to give reality to the *uses* of arithmetical and geometrical concepts and skills.

The second we call the **contextual**, which is ensuring the concept or skill is seeded into other topics and other activities. For instance, in geography the class may have a lesson on longitude and latitude, using the map of part of the world to illustrate the concept and for the pupils to practise the skill of using it: specific. Another time the study of a part of the world will bring in that contextual concept.

Teachers need a judicious balance. Sometimes content comes in as a sideline, sometimes it is the central focus. Sometimes we are saying specifically, 'For the next three weeks we will look at South Asian culture'. Other times when we are teaching something about mathematics, geography, or science, a little touch of a culture is deliberately placed in the context. Thus each course in the school, whilst planned coherently, could be encouraged to include cultural aspects and to be planned within whole-school policies. This contextual mode could be called 'arts across the curriculum'.

Curriculum delivery

The mechanical-sounding term 'delivery' puts off many people, especially in as creative and sensitive an aspect of the secondary school as the arts. The term, though, is useful in helping us review and plan the division of the work we do with pupils in the arts. 'Curriculum' is best

Whole-school curriculum planning for the arts

thought of as the *overall* planning of content, skills, and attitudes the school hopes to enable its pupils to develop. 'Subject' confuses as it has two meanings: a philosophical division of knowledge and skills and a division of the school (or college or university) time. These are not necessarily co-terminus, and curriculum divisions made for intellectual planning purposes can rarely be taught and learnt only in that course.

It would be easier if we had a more practical nomenclature, using the term 'course' for the separately taught programmes of study in secondary schools and keeping 'subject' only for the intellectual divisions of whole-school planning. The National Curriculum legislation is absolutely clear that there is no central control of the arrangements of content into courses, and the legislative headings ('subjects') are QCA *planning* divisions only, not instructions on how to slide between the different school courses. This is particularly important in the arts as the National Curriculum subject planning divisions specifically include the following aspects of the arts:

- National Curriculum 'English' includes 'drama' and 'media';
- National Curriculum Physical Education includes 'dance';
- 'Architecture' is mentioned only in Key Stage 1 'Art';
- 'Design Technology' has some aesthetic reference and includes 'Textiles';
- 'Citizenship' includes 'cultural issues'.

As Section 3 of Chapter 1 set out, there is no statutory control of the division into courses nor of the whole, overall content of the school curriculum. Somewhere, somehow, from time to time, it has to *include* the contents of the National Curriculum 'programme of study'. However, *a school can divide the richness of the arts into 'courses' in any way it judges fit.*

There could be for instance:

'Arts'	all in one many-faceted course
'Performing Arts'	Music, Dance, and Drama
'Art and Design'	Visual Arts and Design Technology
'Art', 'Music', 'English'	Drama and Media
'PE'	Dance

There are many other combinations. It has been strongly argued that many secondary school 'Art' courses are too narrowly defined, a problem exacerbated by the initial National Curriculum emphasis on 'fine art' and technical skill. The specifications for 2000 certainly adumbrated a wider range, yet the National Advisory Committee on Creative and Cultural Education judged:

> There are concerns about the definition of the subject. Visual arts specialists generally argue that the subject should be named art and design, and include craft activities. Currently, art teaching has a strong fine art emphasis, and design and technology a strong manufacturing one. The National Curriculum has imposed a prescriptive model of art education which emphasises technical skill at the expense of creative and conceptual innovation. In art, especially at Key Stages Three and Four, there is very little craft and design. The curriculum focuses predominantly on drawing and painting.
>
> (NACCCE, 1999, p.180)

Similarly, an aspect of arts can be formally located in other courses. Although Ofsted have found that when 'drama' is in the 'English' course it is often limited in scope, it is not impossible to so arrange. As will be explored later in this chapter, small units can be in History, Religion, PSHE, Citizenship, and Languages. Additionally, there will be references to the arts in many other units, even including some Science and Mathematics.

An example is design. In a course which specifically teaches 'Design', examples will be brought in to illustrate the points. There is still a value from design being 'brought into' other contexts to point up something. Too often crucial aspects of a subject involve design, but the design of many common items and the aesthetic aspects of that design are often totally missing from the present curriculum of those subjects in many schools.

The design of books, typography, and binding, and even the technology of a book, such as the 'gatherings' and 'end-papers', are examples of this. The Print Room at the Victoria and Albert Museum, for instance, has a glorious collection of decorative papers, used in publishing as end-papers. (An introduction has been published, V&A, 1985.) Pupils of quite young ages enjoy looking at the title pages, bindings, dust jackets, and page layout – and with a little prompting can compare the styles. The 'English' specifications of the National Curriculum recommend the writing of William Morris. It is rare, though, for his keen interest in typography to be mentioned in schools. Indeed the very term, its techniques, and its vocabulary are hardly present in any part of the curriculum, whether 'Art', 'Design Technology', or 'English'.

Whilst the full range of requirements of the National Curriculum 'Design Technology' must be met, a DT course need not be limited by those requirements and the *art* aspects can be included. The aesthetic has always had a place in 'Technology' departments, but its significance has varied. A central London boys' school that closed in 1980 (Rutherford School) had a 'Technical Department', which was described as 'Engineering, Woodwork, and Technical Drawing'. Its policy stated:

> Whenever possible, stress should be given to the aesthetic aspects of the craft. Boys will be encouraged to think of the function, correct construction and use of materials, and the appearance of an article as closely related aspects of design and not as separate factors. In this respect there must be close correlation with the work of the Art Department.

▰ Routes for delivery

There are five complementary routes for the two modes of delivery described on p.78, and although the first is the major highway the others are also extremely important and should be planned with great care and flair:

(a) specific arts courses;

(b) components in other courses;

(c) the 'home-room', 'pastoral', or 'tutorial' programme;

(d) the communal life of the school;

(e) the school environment.

The five routes of delivery make great demands on a school – teaching in course classrooms requires wide and substantial organisational support, but the proper uses of the other 'routes' requires strong and sensitive school-wide planning and support. A well-devised secondary arts curriculum plans these routes for delivery of the whole arts range in a coherent way. It exploits serendipitous opportunities as they arise, but also locates key concepts, facts, skills, and experiences in the context of each route.

(a) Specific arts courses

The main mode of delivering the curriculum is through the courses which are named in schools as Science, Maths, and so on. That is a very important way, provided that the people in charge of those courses do not close the door to extra content. Some heads of departments in UK schools used to like to say: 'Go away, Headteacher: I am in charge of history so we will do it this way.' Such heads more recently tend to use the National Curriculum content orders as protection.

Yet shaping these courses deserves far more consideration than has taken place. For instance, the English and Welsh statutory orders following the 1988 legislation specifies: 'Music' and 'Art' as separate 'subjects'; literature, drama, and media within the subject 'English': dance within 'Physical Education'; and architecture as a non-statutory 'example' in 'Art'. Any decision is awkward, but this is especially so. The Northern Ireland statutory orders, devised a little time later, used a broad overview, 'aesthetic aspects', and are therefore far more openly flexible.

The repetitions of combinations of the arts into specific courses is vast. There can be a judicious blending of closely focused and broad. Thus, for twelve-, thirteen-, and fourteen-year-olds at one school there is a course called 'Performing Arts', with specialist teaching of dance, drama (or theatre), and music. Visual Arts is a separate course, as is Textiles, which is often taught as an aspect of Design Technology, itself more of an art than many would allow.

How to divide and how to link is a difficult decision. One of the key axioms of curriculum planning is that every decision to separate requires a bridge, but that every joining requires an opportunity for separate focus. Vivid, vigorous, specialist art-form courses work well with specialist teachers, but have to have an underlying curriculum that weaves the themes of concepts, skills, and attitudes through the separate courses. Section 3 of Chapter 4 gives more detail.

Sometimes, divisions between 'the arts' lose important interconnections, such as the relationship between Tudor painting and music, Islamic architecture and clothing, Eric Gill's typography and sculpture. The National Curriculum 'English' specifications admirably include the great Bengali philosopher and artist Rabindranath Tagore. However, he is noted only as a poet and not as a visual artist, dramatist, novelist, singer, or composer – all of which he was.

We do not always support the managing of the arts in broader courses. 'Drama' illuminates 'English', but can be lost within it, as can 'Media'. Music, Drama, and Dance complement each other. The relationship of 'textiles' to other courses is difficult: is it an art or a technology? The relationship of the art of design to 'Design Technology' similarly requires care.

The 'personal growth' or 'reaction' model for education in the arts rejected not only 'cultures', as every meeting with an art was seen merely as a one-night-stand, but also rejected an interest in the artistic world – techniques, biography, economics, individual skills, and social pressure – that led to the manifestation of art. The rejection of the 'critical biography' and the mechanics of art gives an unintended message that works of art come fully formed from the creator, like the packaged vegetables of the super-market, without a touch of the earth in which they were grown.

It is very important to consider the curriculum purpose of the Key Stage 3 Design Technology course. Appreciation of the made world, that is the full range of the artefacts, is the core of the Design Technology course. The key learning aim is for pupils to be able to see each of the components of the made world, and consider:

Why is it as it is, and how could it have been otherwise?

This involves knowledge about and understanding of purposes, materials, structures, cultural understanding, often energy mechanisms, aesthetic taste, and the then human, societal life. This 'seeing', understanding, and appreciating of artefacts of humanity is the process referred to in the first statutory National Curriculum orders as 'disassembling'. It has a clearly artistic component. The range of 'made objects' (that is 'artefacts') will include furniture, architecture, jewellery, domestic devices, and the constructional engineering of bridges.

(b) Components in other courses

However the secondary curriculum is divided into courses, most will have an arts dimension at least occasionally and sometimes very significantly, and the same is true of the 'special focuses' of Key Stages 1 and 2.

There should be a very wide range of activities, not only in courses named as the arts, but in other courses such as RE, mathematics, science, and humanities. The opportunities for focusing on an aspect of the arts to highlight a key point in an apparently non-art course are huge, and deeply enriching.

In UK history, the arts are often missed out. For example, in one course the European eighteenth-century town is described, but not the eighteenth-century architecture that made up that town. The balance of the couplet, and the structure of the music was echoed in the invention of the terrace, which in aesthetic form expressed a social notion of the world in which urbane and urban had inter-related meanings. Hardly any aspect of history in any culture does not have an artistic dimension.

The National Curriculum History 'Victorian' requirement in Key Stage 2, the industrial revolution, both world wars, and many aspects of earlier history are well evoked in ballads, both from the oral traditions and popular, musical-hall song-writers. Central government once recommended the use of folk songs in schools, which provided 'an expression in the idiom of the people of their joys and sorrows, their unaffected patriotism, their zest for sport and the simple pleasures of country life'. However, that was the Board of Education in 1805! More recently, central government appears to see no connection between songs and history. In fact, many songs are very pointed, such as:

- Technological History: Humphrey Hardfeature's Descriptions of Cast-Iron Inventions, 1822
- Poor Law Amendment Act of 1834 and the Workhouses: A dialogue and song on the Starvation Poor Law Bill, 1884.

Similarly, consider the study of the Tudor period in the UK, which must, at least briefly, include Tudor building and music. The timber building can well be compared with Yoruba architecture in Nigeria. Both peoples were working with timber, and coming to some similar technical solutions (for example jointing) and some similar aesthetic effects. To listen to a range of the deeply distinctive music of the age is also an essential aspect of history. For instance, the period is really conveyed to pupils by what has been evocatively described as 'the austerely beautiful Tudor polyphony echoing through lofty naves'.

Similarly dance can be linked illuminatingly to History. The Cheshire Dance Workshop has shown how aspects of dance can be taught, as for example in different aspects of Egyptian culture. You go through history in most British schools without the word dance ever being mentioned, as if people did not dance in other eras and other cultures. In many cultures in many periods dance has been a major part of shaping that culture and in assisting group coherence in communities. We need to understand specific styles and genres in different traditions, which can illuminate aspects of religious study, geography and history.

No study of religion in any faith can afford to ignore its use of the arts to explore, interpret, and represent. The calculations of Pythagoras's 'golden mean' underlie Greek, Romans, and eighteenth-century European architecture. The major renaissance Gothic cathedral at Rheims in France was designed using Islam's interpretation of Greek geometry. Each of the faiths has many artistic manifestations, so Religious Education courses must contain visual and architectural artistic points, whether studying Christian, Jewish, Hindu, or Islamic faiths.

Science has its aesthetic aspects: the discovery of DNA, for instance, had a crucial aesthetic component as one of the co-discoverers stressed: 'What I think is overlooked in such arguments is the intrinsic beauty of the DNA double helix.' (Crick, 1989, p.76) He recounts the co-discoverer, James Watson, giving a talk about the discovery of the double helix form of DNA soon after their publication at a scientific club dinner: 'When he came to sum up he was quite overcome and at a loss for words. He gazed at the model, slightly bleary-eyed. All he could manage to say was "It's so beautiful, you see, so beautiful!" But then, of course, it was.' (Crick, 1989, p.79). The aesthetic interest of Crick and Watson was significant in this, the greatest biological discovery of the twentieth century.

The next section gives more examples of aspects of the arts in other courses and in tutorial sessions. Whole-school planning should be as wide-ranging and open as possible, incorporating the National Curriculum components, but not being constrained by them. Then the routes of delivery should be explored, with the strong detailing of 'aspects of the arts in other courses and tutorial sessions' (Chapter 3, Section 4) and 'other curriculum content in arts courses' (Chapter 3, Section 5).

3.4 Aspects of the arts in other courses and tutorial sessions

The arts are part of, influence, and can enlighten the other subjects in the school curriculum. They can also help to initiate, encourage and sustain the elements of creativity across the curriculum. In turn, the arts are enhanced by this interchange, enabling students and their teachers to find new ways of expressing themselves.

Take, for instance, drawing. Campaign for Drawing director Sue Grayston Ford explains that this skill is one of the most effective tools to create understanding, expression, and innovation not just across the arts but in the sciences and humanities as well. 'Whether it is a science diagram illustrating physical processes, a map showing weather patterns, or the partner to creative writing, a drawing can help people plan, think and communicate.' Drawing is an example of how the concept of visual literacy should be set alongside those of verbal literacy and numeracy. This will ensure that children acquire skills and perception that will benefit their whole education.

Each of the art forms, such as art and design, dance, drama, and music, plus architecture, film, and photography, can readily be seen, and used, to enhance learning and understanding in other subjects. This cannot be a prescriptive exercise. Rather it is related to the innovative approach of individual teachers as they explore the links between their own specialist subject, particular art forms and experiences, and (just as significantly) their own artistic or cultural skills and interests. Here, though, are some examples to highlight the potential of the arts to inform other subject areas and to help provide that elusive broadness and balance in today's schooling.

History

Many movements in history are frequently taught without reference to their aesthetic aspects, whether minor or major. For instance, the design and construction of the Crystal Palace in 1851 should not be considered only in relationship to Victorian commercial growth, the Great Exhibition, or even the use of cast iron. What made it so beautiful for the visitors of its age, and those many who admired it after its re-erection in Sydenham? This was a marvellous example of public art in the community – the art of iron and glass. How many primary schools have taught a unit of Tudor history (required in Key Stage 2 by the National Curriculum) without giving the children the opportunity of listening to any Tudor music in authentic recordings? How many pupils have reached a greater understanding of the First World War through listening to the songs and reading the poetry written during this period?

The choice of dramatic texts for performance can, of course, sometimes be made particularly to involve historical and social research and to give human reality to an historical theme. Such a play, in conjunction with a magazine-type programme and an exhibition, can be the culmination of a co-operative run of work. John Hipkin's *The Peterloo Massacre* (Heinemann, 1968) is one such text, already performed by many schools. The haunting scene in which the survivors pick up their dead and wounded friends and relatives long remains in the minds of spectators and (for this is specially the point) allows or even forces the performers to experience the historical event.

An example with a more 'literary' bias is the adaptation of Crabbe's poem *Peter Grimes* (Marland, 1969). The theme is the unfeeling reactions of the Borough folk and the tragedy of a man caught up in his own cruelty – both highlighted by the apprenticeship system of the late eighteenth century. The pupils' historical reading included many examples of contemporary documents (such as excerpts from the Select Committee before the House of Commons). The 'English' reading included not only Crabbe's original *Peter Grimes* poem but also his *Ellen Orford* (both in his collection of 1810, *The Borough*). On a smaller scale, a primary Year 5 class enacted from a script the story of Aeneas for their study of Greek mythology.

Religious Education

The Religious Education curriculum derived from SACRE policies in many areas has little or no focus on the place of art in the various religions taught. This is a strange gap as each of the major religions of the world has its own inherent approach to and use of many aspects of art. For instance, the great Anglican, Percy Dearmer, who devised and edited the major revision of the Anglican hymnal, stated in his published lectures *The Art of Public Worship*, in 1919: 'There can be no public worship without art. However, bad it is, the art is there.' He elaborated: 'Whatever we do, we cannot avoid the practice of art; but we can avoid beauty, as we can avoid truth. We can have all our arts bad, and sink our worship in misery and humiliation.' (Gray, 2000, p.143)

How often in the RE courses' coverage of the traditions of Roman Catholic and Anglican worship are the artistic aspects of architecture, sculpture, stained glass, poetry, and music included? The Christian traditions are still powerful even in our largely secular age. Christian art has gloried in its diversity, with Romanesque, Gothic, Byzantine, and Renaissance styles sharply different. In Islamic art, on the other hand, a definite style and repertory of motifs were used very early to create an association between idea and faith. The Renaissance search for the new and the unfamiliar still lies deep in the work of Western European artists.

Islam should be included in all school RE courses, and is in most. However, Islamic art is often not seen as relevant. Rarely is the Islamic use of geometry included. Islamic art creates its appeal by subtle variations of detail within a unity. The ancient Greek emphasis on 'the golden mean' was absorbed and given fresh lift in Islam. Plato's vision (in *Philebus*) of geometry is essential to an understanding of Islam:

> I do not now intend of beauty, of shapes, what most people would expect, such as that of living creatures or pictures, but straight lines and curves and the surfaces or solid forms produced out of these by lathes and rulers and squares. These things are not beautiful relatively, like other things, but always and naturally beautiful.

Virtually all Islamic design can be understood through Greek geometry and the uses of 'the golden mean'. A detailed analysis of Islamic arch design stresses:

> Islamic architecture has, in common with Medieval Christian architecture of the great cathedrals, an understanding of the power, significance and beauty of geometry that transcends its purely mathematical nature.

(Azzam & Critchlow, 1997, p.5)

Graphicacy

This skill has not had the support of 'graphicacy across the curriculum' as 'literacy' has. Whilst it is not so important or pervasive, it is an art-related skill, a subset of our outline of 'Graphic Design' in Chapter 2, Section 3. In many studies, graphic representation conveys ideas and facts. The subset of 'Graphic Design' is the ability to explore, interpret, and convey analyses, numerical patterns, and ideas through diagrams, graphs, maps, and sketches. Several school courses use graphicacy from time to time, but very few schools have a planned overall approach, using specific tuition and contextual support. An overall survey of the HMI inspections of schools for 1982 to 1986 found that graphicacy 'formed a part of teaching and learning in several subjects in most schools, though its development was not always explicitly acknowledged as an aim' (HMI, 1988, p.26). The report found:

> Often, though not always, CDT, technical drawing and design made significant contributions. Pupils frequently were able to represent ideas imaginatively using a wide range of techniques from rough sketches to plans which made use of grids. In those mathematics and geography departments in which consideration of spatial concepts played a part in the work, pie charts, histograms, graphs, maps of all kinds and tables were often used to good effect. Work in fabrics often involved both design activities and, less frequently, the making of patterns for garments. Too often, however, the use made of diagrams and drawing in other subjects, notably history and religious education, was confined to copying from books or worksheets, and while this improved the appearance and presentation of the work, it did little to extend pupils' thinking about and understanding of the central material of the lesson.
>
> (HMI, 1988, p.27)

Whilst this subset of 'Graphic Design' might not be thought of as 'art', it is a significant example of an aspect of visual art which plays a part in other courses. Many aspects of a pupil's overall learning benefit if the visual art element is recognised and planned for. Specific teaching should be given according to a whole-school plan in an agreed course. Especially significant to the theme of this book is the HMI suggestion that 'the use' should not be 'confined to copying'. A subset of the overall approach to the arts should be 'graphicacy across the curriculum'.

Tutorial sessions in secondary schools

The tutor's remit is so wide and so important that it is seriously difficult to undertake fully. As we have said of *The Art of the Tutor*: 'At the heart of the work of a secondary school is enabling a child to become a student and more fully a person.' The tutor is the core of the secondary school. Her or his task has to relate to the overall ethos of the school, and to help the tutees understand themselves and others. In the next

Aspects of the arts in other courses and tutorial sessions

section (3.6) of this chapter we show some of the ways in which arts courses support Personal and Social Development (PSD). The converse is also true: tutorial sessions should fairly often both use the arts and support them.

Most often a tutor will introduce and explore an aspect of personal and social development by referring to wise sayings, research, anecdote, and pupil discussion. Occasionally a work of art should be used to heighten sensitivity, extend experience, and increase empathy. This may be a passing reference or a major presentation with the PSD aspect highlighted by discussion. Here are some examples:

- A year 8 tutor group was considering aspects of family partings and adoption. They played on CD the song *Oklahoma*, sung by the highly skilled Billy Gilman, a thirteen-year-old American singer. This was a very moving as well as beautiful song that led to a discussion at a deep level (Williams and Allen, 2000).

- An exercise for Year 8 tutor groups on the theme of 'Friends can help you out' was built around a three-page extract from a novel about a girl at school in London: *Sumitra* by Rukshana Smith (1982). The extract was followed by assignments, including:

  Everybody tries to be very kind and welcoming, but they give Sumitra extra worries at the same time! What happens when

  – *the tall, confident boy leaves her in the headteacher's office?*

  – *the headteacher leaves her in her new classroom?*

  – *the new teacher, Miss Watkins, introduces her to Hilary?*

  – *Sumitra hears about special clothes for games?*

  – *Miss Watkins has a little talk with her at the end of the day?*

  Sumitra tries to learn quickly and she does her best to adapt to this strange new place. Luckily she has Hilary who's been asked to look after her for these first few bewildering days. Hilary's job is important because Sumitra's happiness might depend on how well Hilary takes her around, introduces her to others in the Tutor Group, shows her where to go, and how things are done.

  (Marsh, 1989, p.32)

- A Year 6 in a primary school were read in assembly Rabindranath Tagore's satirical story *The King's Parrot* on the theme of schooling and the individual (Tagore, 1988, p.77).

- Pupils in Year 5 dressed in traditional Irish clothing and danced two folk dances as part of the theme of 'differences between people'.

Although the pastoral aspect of primary school classes is more woven in by the class teacher to the 'subjects', as in the secondary school tutorial sessions, arts can be well used.

Encouraging creativity

The arts can be united with other subjects in mutually beneficial encounters through the development of creativity and teaching of thinking skills. Creativity extends across all subjects, but art can be a key catalyst in its development. Much work has gone into these issues, notably by the Qualifications and Curriculum Authority (QCA), since the publication of the National Advisory Committee on Creative and Cultural Education report *All Our Futures: Creativity, culture & education* (NACCCE, 1999).

A second report by the think-tank Demos called *The Creative Age: knowledge and skills for the new economy* (Seltzer and Bentley, 1999) has also informed the debate on approaches to defining and developing creativity. The two reports have much in common, and both have fed into the QCA's working groups and policymaking on creativity and on the arts.

NACCCE favours a democratic, as opposed to elitist, concept of creativity. This is one which recognises the potential for creative achievement in all fields of human activity, and the capacity for such achievements in the many and not the few. It gives four characteristics of creative processes:

- they involve thinking or behaving imaginatively;
- they are purposeful, that is, directed to achieve an objective;
- they must generate something original;
- they produce valued outcomes.

This leads to the definition of creativity as: 'Imaginative activity fashioned so as to produce outcomes that are both original and of value'.

Creative ability is developed through practical application, involving particular skills in each type of work ('domain specific') yet with general qualities which are relevant across all disciplines. Creativity is therefore not a single power but multidimensional.

Creative processes usually involve an initial period of giving shape to an idea (drafting), developing 'successive approximations', then refining the final version. Creative activity comprises a complex combination of controlled and non-controlled elements, unconscious and conscious mental processes, non-directed and directed thought, intuitive and rational calculation.

Two fundamental dynamics drive these creative processes:

- Freedom and control: The freedom to experiment and the discipline of acquiring and using specific skills, knowledge and understanding are mutually dependent elements at the heart of the creative process.
- Creativity and culture: Creativity is not a wholly individual process. Creative achievement always draws from the ideas and achievements of other people. Just as different modes of thinking interact in a single mind, individual creativity is affected by dialogue with others. Thus, creative development is intimately related to cultural development.

While creative education can enhance problem-solving abilities, creativity and problem-solving are not the same thing. Not all creative thinking is directed to solving problems; not all problems require a creative solution. Creative thinkers find problems as yet unimagined and lead to new horizons. Young people need more opportunities to define problems for themselves, to generate ideas, to look at the world in different ways.

For Demos, creativity is not an individual characteristic or innate talent, but 'the application of knowledge and skills in new ways to achieve a valued goal'. This requires:

- the ability to identify new problems rather than depend on others to do so;
- the ability to transfer knowledge across different contexts;
- a belief in learning as incremental in which repeated attempts (that is, making mistakes) eventually leads to success;
- the capacity to focus attention on pursuing a goal.

Creativity occurs when learners interact with environments that offer:

- trusting relationships in which people are prepared to take risks;
- the freedom of action to make a range of choices;
- a variety of contexts in which to apply skills;
- the right balance between skills and challenge;
- the interactive exchange of knowledge and ideas; and
- opportunities to achieve concrete outcomes and change how things are done.

Demos argues that the curriculum should focus on depth of understanding and breadth of application rather than content in order to nurture 'independent, creative and rigorous lifelong learners'. In order to do this:

- Curriculum content and time should be reduced by half.
- The six 'key skills' of communication, application of numbers, working with others, use of ICT, problem solving, and improving one's own learning and performance, should be redefined as six clusters of skills. These can be described in terms of: self-organisation, including forming and articulating goals; personal and inter-personal relationships; information management; risk management; disciplinary and inter-disciplinary knowledge; and reflection and evaluation. They should be built into all areas of education from birth to nineteen.
- The out-of-school learning infrastructure, such as study support, should be developed to provide every pupil with opportunities for project-based and placement learning.
- Teachers should be rewarded for creativity and innovation.

The report also identifies a further set of skills which derive from the need to manage risk:

- futures thinking: being able to imagine and analyse different future scenarios and their implications;
- decision-making: being able to think through the available options, and make clear decisions about the best one;
- stress management: knowing how to cope with tension and direct one's energy in healthy ways;
- learning from failure: being able to translate one's mistakes or shortcomings into opportunities for learning.

Thinking skills

In his North of England Conference speech in January 2000, the then Education Secretary David Blunkett announced a professional development pilot programme for secondary teachers to learn how to teach higher-order thinking skills through their subjects. He explained:

I have been very impressed by the growing evidence in this country, and abroad, of the impact on standards of systematic and disciplined approaches to the

Aspects of the arts in other courses and tutorial sessions 93

teaching of higher order thinking skills. The most impressive work in this country has been through the CASE (Cognitive Acceleration through Science Education) project, developed at King's College London. Pupils involved in the project have performed substantially better at GCSE than equivalent pupils not involved in the programme. There is now a similar successful programme in maths. It is not about some loosely defined or woolly approach to study skills.

(Blunkett, 2000)

It is about the ability to analyse and make connections, to use knowledge effectively, to solve problems individually and to think creatively. It is about developing mental strategies to take on both academic and wider challenges. Above all, the evidence – not just from the CASE project – shows that the systematic teaching of thinking skills raises standards. The new enthusiasm for thinking skills stems from a DfEE-commissioned review and evaluation of approaches for developing pupils' thinking. *From Thinking Skills to Thinking Classrooms* by Dr Carol McGuinness of Queen's University Belfast was published in April 1999 (available free from DfEE Publications on 0845 60 222 60; fax 0845 60 333 60; e-mail dfee@prologistics.co.uk). The review looked at:

- what is understood by 'thinking skills' and their role in the learning process;
- the effectiveness of current approaches to developing pupils' thinking;
- how teachers might integrate thinking skills into their teaching within subject areas and across the curriculum;
- the role of ICT in promoting thinking skills; and
- the current and future direction of research and how it might translate into classroom practice.

The QCA primary and secondary handbooks for the revised National Curriculum state:

By using thinking skills pupils can focus on 'knowing how' as well as 'knowing what' – learning how to learn.

The QCA then identifies five types of thinking skills: 'information processing, reasoning, enquiry, creative thinking, evaluation'. It also importantly stresses that the thinking skills 'complement the key skills: 'communication, application of number, information technology, working with others, improving own learning and performance, problem solving'. (QCA, 1999, pp.22–4).

Developing creativity requires effective collaboration over the arts between teachers across all subjects. This is most valuable if begun in initial training and pursued through continuing professional development. A key proving ground for such an approach is the STAR project in the Wednesbury Education Action Zone. This project brings together teacher training providers, local schools, and arts organisations to embed the arts within the training of every teacher (see the Appendix).

Conclusion

The widely perceived (but not actually intended or statutorily required) sharp division of the 'subject' teaching in school 'courses' has tended to drive out references to any aspect of the arts. Dr Nicholas Tate lecturing on 'The Contribution of Design and Technology to the Curriculum' stressed: 'Education in technology is aimed at familiarising the pupils with those aspects of technology which are significant to the proper understanding of culture.' He asked as an example, 'Do we have a curriculum which encourages us to do the kind of work in architecture and the built environment . . . which is very much about that interaction of technology, culture, and values?' (Tate, 1996, p.7).

Teachers of subject courses other than the arts should not feel inhibited to mention their own interest and love of an art. A Science teacher used the last three minutes of a Year 10 lesson to share his pleasure that he was going to see *Rigoletto* at an opera house that evening. A history teacher gave a sixth-former a personal gift: the *Penguin Book of Contemporary Verse*. All these examples are perfectly proper and supportive of the arts – but some interpretations of post 1988 legislation wrongly prohibit references to the arts in other 'subjects'. Appropriate inclusion strengthens both the whole-school arts curriculum and the other courses.

3.5 Other curriculum content in arts courses

Introduction

In this section of the chapter, we shall indicate some of the key aspects of the whole-school curriculum which can and should be woven subtly but powerfully into the arts courses (in alphabetical order):

- Economics
- History

- ICT
- Literacy
- Occupations
- Personal and Social Development
- Technology.

Economics

From the points of view of society, organisation, and management, and the world's economies, an understanding of the financial costs and contribution of the arts is important. This requires some overview lessons, indicating how funds are achieved for materials, overheads, staff, marketing, and artists' salaries. It requires a broad picture of different countries and different periods, from, say, Tudor England to the late nineteenth century, and across different countries today. Local arts organisations should be included, and a theatre and an art gallery, could be explained even to quite early years.

Certain of the arts should be given a detailed analysis, for example what does a full professional dance company cost in terms of dancers, scenery, orchestra, back stage, management, and publicity?

Some indication of media costs should be included, for instance typical advertising rates. At the start of this century, for instance, a full-page advertisement in the following UK newspapers cost the sums shown:

Newspaper	Advertising rate
Independent	£15,000
Guardian	£16,275
Evening Standard (London)	£11,715
Daily Mail	£40,000
The Times	£23,500
Daily Telegraph	£41,500
The Mirror	£33,300

What are the salaries of different artists employed in organisations? How do free-lance artists earn their income and pay tax? For instance, briefly which expenses can they claim against tax? When and on what items is VAT charged?

What are the country's national policies on arts funding and how have they changed over the years? What does this school spend on stage lighting, graphic design, photography, visiting performing musicians? Then there needs to be a cross-cultural international perspective:

Asian countries, America, a European country – how are the costs of the arts spread between audiences and government?

Whilst these economic aspects may only have a small part in the curriculum delivery, they are valuable for the broad societal understanding of finance, and give a detailed sense of realism about the practical workings of the arts. Even primary school classes should have broad outlines, and Key Stage 3 classes some detail.

History

In the previous section we have argued that the specific History course in primary and secondary schools should have a much greater and deeper inclusion of the arts. Conversely, the arts courses should contribute more than they currently do to each pupil's sense of period, development, and change over the years in different cultures. For instance, for Music the National Curriculum QCA document includes:

> Cultural development, *through helping pupils recognise how music influences and reflects the way people think and feel, relating music to the time and place in which it was created and performed, and through analysing, evaluating and reflecting on music from contrasting traditions and identifying how and why some aspects change or stay the same.*
>
> (DfEE and QCA 1999, *Music*, p.8)

It would help the success both of this important ambition and of whole-school teaching if the music class supported wider historical teaching, for instance:

- backing medieval music with reference to the church and state; also including architecture;
- supporting steel-band music teaching with the broad history of the settlement of the Caribbean islands and cultural interaction;
- placing the growth of the symphony orchestra in nineteenth-century European history.

The QCA guidance includes 'cultural diversity' for both Music and Art and Design. The same is true of the other arts. One effective way of meeting this is to mention history in introductions and explanations, and sometimes even to make history the core of a lesson or half a lesson. For instance, cultural diversity is well highlighted by such history as:

- The steel band – with African, South American, and European roots, and the bamboo-tamboo predecessor;

- Architectural juxtapositions – for example the 1626 St James's Church and its neighbour Lutyens' 1922 Midland Bank in Piccadilly, London W1;
- Viking design, such as a brooch in reproductions;
- The Umayyads – the foundations of Islamic art in the seventh century (c.f. Hillenbrand, 1999).

Most nineteenth-century ballads have a strong narrative and descriptive power and move pupils by their personal involvement. Many also have a significant social history element. Pupils know that a 'School Board Officer' today is an 'Education Welfare Officer' and they are taught nineteenth-century urban living conditions in History including the 1870 School Board.

The following ballad is by George R. Sims, playwright, novelist, and journalist as well as one of the most famous ballad-mongers. Published in the 1870s and 1880s, his ballads were widely performed and very popular (Sims, 1968, p.141). *The Magic Wand* really makes pupils think and feel:

The Magic Wand: A School Board Officer's Story

Horrible dens, sir, aren't they?
   This is one of my daily rounds
It's here, in these awful places,
   That child-life most abounds.
We ferret from roof to basement
   In search of our tiny prey;
We're down on their homes directly
   If they happen to stop away.

Knock at the door! Pooh, nonsense!
   They wouldn't know what it meant.
Come in and look about you;
   They'll think you're a School Board gent.
Did you ever see such hovels?
   Dirty, and damp, and small.
Look at the rotten flooring,
   Look at the filthy wall.

That's lucky – the place is empty,
   The whole of the family's out.
This is one of my fav'rite cases:
   Just give a glance about.
There's a father and four young children,
   And Sally the eldest's eight;

They're horribly poor – half starving–
   And they live in a shocking state.

The father gets drunk and beats them,
   The mother she died last year:
There's a story about her dying
   I fancy you'd like to hear.
She was one of our backward pupils,
   Was Sally the eldest child –
A poor little London blossom
   The alley had not defiled.

She was on at the Lane last winter –
   She played in the pantomime;
A lot of our School Board children
   Get on at the Christmas time.
She was one of a group of fairies,
   And her wand was the wand up there –
There, in the filthy corner
   Behind the broken chair.

The gilt of the star has faded,
   And the tinsel's peeled away;
But once, in the glaring lime-light,
   It gleamed like a jewelled spray.
A fairy's wand in a lodging
   In a slum like this looks queer;
But you'll guess why they let her keep it
   When you know how the wand came here.

Her mother was ill that winter,
   Her father, the drunken sot,
Was spending his weekly earnings
   And all that the fairy got.
The woman lay sick and moaning,
   Dying by slow degrees
Of a cruel and wasting fever
   That rages in dens like these.

But night after night went Sally,
   Half starved, to the splendid scene
Where she waved a wand of magic
   As a Liliput fairy queen.
She stood in the 'Land of Shadows'
   Where a demon worked his spell,

At a wave of her wand he vanished,
    And the scene was changed as well.

She's a couple of lines to utter,
    Which bade the gloom give away
To the 'Golden Home of Blisses
    In the Land of the Shining Day.'
She gazed on the limelight splendours
    That grew as she waved her wand,
And she thought of the cheerless cellar
    Old Drury's walls beyond.

And when, in her ragged garments,
    No longer a potent fay,
She knelt by the wretched pallet
    Where her dying mother lay.
She thought, as she stooped and kissed her,
    And looked in the ghastly face,
Of the wand that could change a dungeon
    To a sweet and lovely place.

She was only a wretched outcast,
    A waif of the London slums;
It's little of truth and knowledge
    To the ears of such children comes.
She fancied her wand was truly
    Possessed of a magic charm,
That it punished the wicked people,
    And shielded the good from harm.

Her mother grew slowly weaker,
    The depth of the winter came,
And the teeth of the biting weather
    Seized on the wasted frame.
And Sally, who saw her sinking,
    Came home from the Lane one night
With her shawl wrapped over something,
    And her face a ghostly white.

She had hidden the wand and brought it,
    The wand that could do so much;
She crept to the sleeping woman,
    Who moved not at her touch.
She stooped to hear her breathing,

> It was, O, so fair and low;
> Then, raising her wand, she waved it,
> Like a fairy, to and fro.
>
> Her well-known lines she uttered,
> That bade the gloom give way
> To 'The Golden Home of Blisses
> In the Land of Shining Day.'
> She murmured, 'O mother, dearest,
> You shall look on the splendid scene!'
> While a man from the playhouse watched her
> Who'd followed the fairy queen.
>
> He thought she had stolen something,
> And brought it away to sell,
> He had followed her home and caught her
> And then he'd a tale to tell.
> He told how he watched her waving
> The wand by her mother's bed,
> O'er a face where the faint grey shadows
> Of the last long sleep had spread.
>
> She's still at the school, is Sally,
> And she's heard of the Realms of Light;
> So she clings to the childish fancy
> That entered her head that night.
> She says that her poor sick mother
> By her wand was charmed away
> From earth to the Home of Blisses
> In the Land of Eternal Day.

Whilst pressures of time, teacher knowledge, and teaching resources will of course limit the scope and detail possible, each of the arts courses should not only use History, but also support wider historical understanding.

▰ Information and Communications Technology

ICT development in pupils should be supported in all courses. Whereas many courses have only administrative and research uses for ICT, the arts have a strong creative use as well.

The *National Curriculum Handbooks* require that in the School Curriculum for Key Stages 1 to 4:

1. Pupils should be given opportunities to apply and develop their ICT capability through the use of ICT tools to support their learning in all subjects.

2. Pupils should be given opportunities to support their work by being taught to:

    a find things out from a variety of sources, synthesising the information to meet their needs and developing an ability to question its accuracy, bias and plausibility.

    b develop their ideas using ICT tools to amend and refine their work and enhance its quality and accuracy.

    c exchange and share information, both directly and through electronic media.

    d review, modify and evaluate their work reflecting critically on its quality, as it progresses.

(DfEE and QCA, 1999, primary, p.39, secondary, p.41)

However, the National Curriculum description of ICT virtually ignores the artistic, creative, aesthetic aspects of ICT. The arts world should meet the National Curriculum requests for ICT by as many opportunities for 'information-handling' and communication as possible. Additionally, however, a school should use the creative and artistic aspects of ICT not only to meet the 'cross curriculum' requirements of the National Curriculum but also as an artistic technical ingredient in itself. For instance, in music two comprehensive school teachers have stressed:

> Within the realm of the music curriculum it seems clear that information and communication technologies (ICT) can be used in two ways. They can function as tools to facilitate models of composition extrinsic to the technology itself (for example, to use MIDI and samplers to emulate a traditional instrumental piece). Or they can be used to generate an entirely new model of composition practice, one that allows a greater exploration of sound itself. The Reflecting Others project falls clearly into the second of these types.

(Savage and Challis, 2001, p.20)

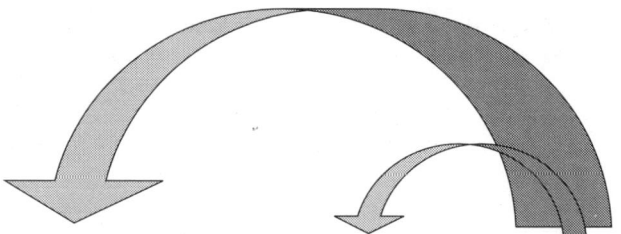

STARTING POINT - EXPERIMENT - SELECT - STRUCTURE - EVALUATE/REVISE

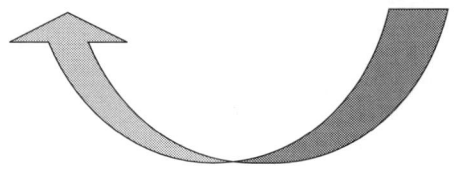

A key project initiated by the Aldeburgh Festival in a Suffolk Comprehensive School and with below-eighteen inmates of a local prison was described in Chapter 2. The musical aspect focused on the use of ICT for composition:

> A specific compositional process was an important element within the project. This process has been extracted from discussions with electroacoustic composers, particularly Mike Challis, and is a simple, five-staged process. It consists of:

> Pupils' work in composition at the school has been framed around this process over the last two years. The Reflecting Others project was neatly divided across the winter break. Prior to Christmas, pupils and young offenders developed creative starting points, experimented and collected appropriate material; after the break they worked on selecting, structuring and evaluating this material.

(Savage and Challis, 2001, p.5)

Digital control can thus be used to 'make music' and a variety of visual artistic effects.

Finally, the 'communication' aspect can readily be used for presentation of drama, poetry, three-dimensional arts, and dance to school, community, and distant audiences.

Literacy

One of the traditional failings of UK schools has been to assume the teaching and learning of English takes place solely in English Literature and English Language. The 1975 national move towards 'Language Across the Curriculum' (Committee of Enquiry, 1975) was effectively taken up in many secondary schools, but was not as deeply woven into teaching as was needed. At the end of the twentieth century there was a fresh government lead in the National Literacy Strategy. There is a new strong encouragement in primary and secondary schools to bring in literacy tuition to all aspects of the curriculum – for language serves and is served by so many aspects.

In the past, some schools have tended to keep virtually all writing out of the arts courses. In fact, some writing assignments, powerfully linked with key concepts and skills of an art, can both deepen the pupils' understanding of the art and at the same time extend their literacy. For instance, a Year 10 class were asked to review a play at the local theatre. They were given the following notes to help them to structure their writing:

Themes
What were the main themes or issues in the play? Choose two that the play made you think about most and explain how the play put them across. What styles or drama forms were used and how?

Costumes
Describe how the costumes helped you understand more about the scene or the characters.

REVIEW
Copy the title, venue and date. Make each box into a paragraph.

Props
How were props used in the telling of the story?

Sound Effects and Lighting
In what ways were these used within the play? Give examples of where they were used and for what purpose.

The Set
Describe the set. Why do you think the playwright set it on top of a high-rise flat?

Acting
Which actors did you think were the best and why? Give reasons to support your answer.

Conclusion
Write a few sentences on your feelings about the play. Would you recommend it? Why?

One Visual Arts Department used the idea for 'Writing Frames'. They specifically shaped these ideas from the aspect of that Visual Arts course: 'Developing non-fiction writing skills in Art and Design Lessons' in six categories.

1. 'Research-type' homework task (tabulated).
2. 'Research-type' homework task (text).
3. Three facts, three opinions research task.
4. Compare and contrast exercise.
5. Project evaluation.
6. Step-by-step instructions.

The second step was thus:

Name _____   Tutor Group _____
Date _____   Project _____

I have been asked to _____

I already know _____

I would like to find out more about _____

I will find out by _____

I learnt that _____

I also learnt that _____

Another interesting fact was _____

However, the most interesting for me was _____

The QCA guidance on *Language at Work in Lessons* (QCA, 2001) gives specific examples on how a course such as the arts can strengthen overall literacy. Essentially those are ways of prompting the appropriate language to stimulate and support the analysis and perception of the theme whilst conversely *using* the themes to sharpen an understanding of aspects of language. Here, for instance, are QCA observations of Year 9 lessons in Art and Design and Music:

Writing examples of effective practice

In subjects:

1. *the need for pupils to develop the ability to write their own coherent texts, sometimes of significant length, is generally recognised and encouraged;*
2. *pupils are helped to organise the content of their writing into complete texts, sometimes through writing frames, which suggest organisation via appropriate connectives, provide structure for paragraphs and lead to closely argued texts.*

Art and Design
Pupils at the beginning of an extended sequence of work are reminded of key terms in image analysis, such as line, tone, texture, pattern, shape, space, colour, and form. They are then asked to make brief notes on Smoking Season *by Hunderstrasser, using each term as a prompt. The key words are displayed prominently in the classroom and in pupils' workbooks. Subsequently, they use these notes to structure paragraphs in an extended piece of writing.*

Music
Pupils in groups study a range of music journalism texts about various bands, musicians, and singers. They are each required to select one musical act and to gather information from a variety of source. They then write their own magazine article in the appropriate style to a given structure, such as introduction, background information, opinion, conclusion.

(QCA, 2001, p.49)

In Year 7 Music classes, QCA observed and virtually recommended as part of an 'introduction to African music':

Subject learning objectives

1. *Increase knowledge of the use of polyrhythms, call and responses, percussion instruments and voices in African music*
2. *Encourage pupils to express and communicate their ideas and the effect that music has on them, and to apply this understanding in composing and performing.*

Literacy objectives

1. *Define and deploy words with precision, including their exact implication in context*
2. *Make brief, clearly organised notes of key points for later use.*

(QCA, 2001, p.21)

This example mentions using words precisely. The arts have a fairly small but important specialist vocabulary. This is a good opportunity to teach how the English vocabulary works, with stems and affixes from Latin and Greek being used for precise terms. Thus the arts vocabulary would be explained not only by giving meaning but also the etymological route to those meanings, learning from and supporting thus the vocabulary outside the arts. The arts teachers need a vocabulary list and agreement about the elements of words to be identified. The teacher's explanation should point out key elements of the word with examples of other well known words that use the same stems and affixes. For example:

acrobatic:	*'acro'* from Greek *'akros'* = highest, top most, outer (e.g. acronym, acrostic)
aural:	*'aur'* from Latin *'auris'* = ear
choreography:	*'chor'* from Greek *'choros'* = dancing place, chorus *'graph'* from Greek *'graphos'* = to write (e.g. autograph, graph, graphic)
collage:	*'colla'* from Greek = 'together'
conduct:	*'con'* from Latin = 'together' *'duc'* from Latin *'ducere'* = lead (e.g. concentric, concord, consanguinity, educate, abduct, duct deduce)
environment:	*'en'* (or *'em'*) from Greek = in *'viron'* from Latin = circle
medieval:	*'med'* from Latin *'medius'* = middle (e.g. median, medium, Mediterranean) *'ev'* from Latin *'aevin'* = age (e.g. coeval, longevity, primeval)
perspective:	*'per'* from Latin for through (e.g. perambulate, perforate, percolate) *'spec'* from Latin *'specere'* and *'spect-'* = to look at (e.g. inspect, prospect, circumspect)
proscenium:	*'pro'* from Greek = before, in front (e.g. progress, prospect, produce) *'scen'* from Greek *'skere'* = scene or stage
symphony:	*'sym'* (also *'syn'* and *'sys'*) from Greek = together (e.g. sympathy, synagogue, synchronise) *'phon'* from Greek = sound or voice (e.g. telephone, microphone, phonetic)

An example from QCA illustrates using vocabulary explanation to sharpen musical listening and thinking:

> The teacher gives out a worksheet with a list of key words, such as melody, tempo, rhythm, timbre, pitch, dynamics and duration, and asks pupils to choose three of these to describe the next piece of music they listen to (Paul Simon's Diamonds on the Soles of her Shoes) and to write brief notes based around these words. Pupils share their responses with the class: 'More upbeat rhythm, more Caribbean'; 'the music has a constant rhythm'; 'the tempo makes you want to dance'; 'the rhythm is different because the choir has been replaced with instruments'

> The teacher links the selection of key words on the worksheet with pupils' immediate application of them in their response to their listening. They use the words as the hooks for their descriptive responses. This continues the process of integrating the musical terminology into their developing expression of personal response. The sharing in the class allows for any difficulties of understanding or differences between specialist and everyday uses of words to be identified and explained.

(QCA, 2001, p.21)

Thus the arts teacher will devise classroom and homework assignments to prompt pupils to use language to explore the arts, and to think and write creatively.

Occupations

The over-emphasised 'personal growth' or 'reaction' model for education in the arts diminished not only 'culture', but also an interest in the artistic world – techniques, biography, economics, individual skills, and social pressure – that forms culture. The rejection of critical biography and the mechanics of art gives an unintended message, that works of art emerge fully formed from the creator – like supermarket shrink-wrapped vegetables, without any trace of the earth in which they were grown.

Instead, some part of the courses should teach the reality of context, that is: how the arts have come to be created, by whom, and from what pressures. Presently in the UK, too many pupils can go through three years of good arts teaching in a secondary school and learn about art but not learn about artists or the support workers and technicians involved in many arts! Are there not ways in which the arts courses can bring in the themes of information technology, controlling stage lights, issues of gender, economics, issues of personal and social education, multicultural issues, language, and careers?

The coverage should include the working life of artists in different circumstances, cultures, and eras. Often in the UK the aspect of occupation has been left out – even sometimes denigrated. If a school has removed the artificer from the artefact, the writer from the written, and the production from the product, the cultural forces that created Indian Moghul painting, Chinese poetry, or African sculpture are invisible. We are extraordinarily poor at including the lives of artists, the technicians, the administrators, and all those 'behind the scenes'.

Biography is a part of the teaching of the arts. We should judiciously bring forward key facts about significant people who have contributed to the arts, usually artists themselves, but sometimes also critics, collectors, and even people of business whose financial skill has been directed to the arts.

It is good if pupils can meet adult artists, both amateur and professional. Sometimes the 'meeting' will be to watch a performance, to hear a talk, or to participate in a workshop. Sometimes personal interviews or informal talks help the pupils realise the simple but important point: artists are people. Art comes from human perceptions, emotions, and hopes.

As an example, the life of a large UK school in one year was artistically enriched by:

1. a Zambian artist in residence;

2. a performance by two young male dancers to a year-group;

3. a visiting string quartet playing in assembly and then talking with and playing to a self-selected group afterwards;

4. exhibitions of professional art, with the purchase of one picture for the school;

5. many visits to theatre, opera, ballet;

6. a talk in assembly by a conductor;

7. literary competitions judged by distinguished published writers;

8. visiting musicians, in some cases performing written-up versions of the pupils' compositions, and bringing music of different cultures together;

9. professional poetry recitals.

Technical aspects should be included not only as part of the pupils' own creation but as an aspect of their general knowledge. How is a film studio organised? What are the techniques of video editing? How do newspaper photographers select angles and focus? How do editors check and alter copy? What is a publicist, a theatrical agent, an arts administrator?

There has often been a view in schools that knowledge about an occupation is of interest and relevance only if the pupil has an interest in 'being one of those'. This has serious consequences for careers education (which is, of course, an aspect of PSD) as a pupil cannot find an interest in an occupation which she or he has not somehow encountered or heard about. It also lessens the growing pupil's knowledge of society and other people's lives. Finally, it has a weakening effect on their understanding of many arts, for instance film, ballet, and lithography.

The place of 'occupations' in the arts courses does not require major planning changes, but the fitting in of background facts, for instance:

1. Include brief career details when mentioning an artist;
2. After viewing a video, re-run the credits, perhaps distribute a paper copy of them, and discuss what the job titles mean;
3. Invite a technician from the theatre world to talk to a class;
4. When there is a big arts news story, ask the class to work out how such stories reach the press;
5. After a visit to a performance, set homework requiring the pupils to list all those workers involved but not performing on stage;
6. Arrange for local visual artists to talk to a class about how they came to be artists and how their painting is funded and fitted into their daily routines.

Although this is a minor aspect of the overall arts curriculum, it supports the wider PSD curriculum and often throws a new light on an art form for the pupils.

Personal and Social Development

Despite the bringing into the National Curriculum of 'Citizenship' as a 'subject', the wider 'pastoral curriculum' requires planning for delivery though all the routes listed on p.81. For the personal and social development of pupils, coverage across the range is especially important, with specific teaching (for example in a PSHE course) complemented by the tutorial work, whole-school ethos, and most of the 'subject' courses. The arts courses have something very special to offer this.

In earlier times there were many examples of personal and social aspects of the curriculum being woven into the specific courses. For the Ragged Schools of the mid-nineteenth-century English towns a song was written to teach in singing lessons the arithmetic of time and the year, and straight morality:

> Sixty seconds make a minute,
>   Time enough to tie my shoe;
> Sixty minutes make an hour,
>   Shall it pass and nought to do?
> Twenty-four hours make a day,
>   Too much time to spend in sleep,
> Too much time to spend in play,
>   For seven days end a week . . .
>
> Fifty-two such weeks will put
>   Near an end to every year
> Days three hundred sixty-five
>   Are the whole that it can share,
> Save in leap-year, when one day
>   Added is to gain lost time: –
> May it not be spent in play
>   Or in any evil crime.
>
> Time is short, we often say;
>   Let us then improve it well,
> That eternally we may
>   Live where happy angels dwell.

As it was strongly put by the Australian Curriculum Corporation in Queensland, Australia in 1991:

> *Effective promotion of the arts in education is dependent on an adequate appreciation of their role in human development.*
>
> (McLeod, 1991, p.iii)

In seeking well-planned ways of bringing PSD into the arts courses, the outstanding work of guidance is the 'framework' in *Passport*, a study funded by the Calouste Gulbenkian Foundation.

> *In secondary schools, PSE/PSHE courses taught by tutors and/or by a specialist team are usually part of designated time in the curriculum. However, PSD cannot be covered by courses alone and opportunities should be sought through other subjects and activities.*
>
> (Lees and Plant, 2000, p.36)

As with all subjects, the arts courses should be reviewed in the light of the school's overall 'Pastoral Curriculum' plan. In the words of *Passport*, there should be three steps:

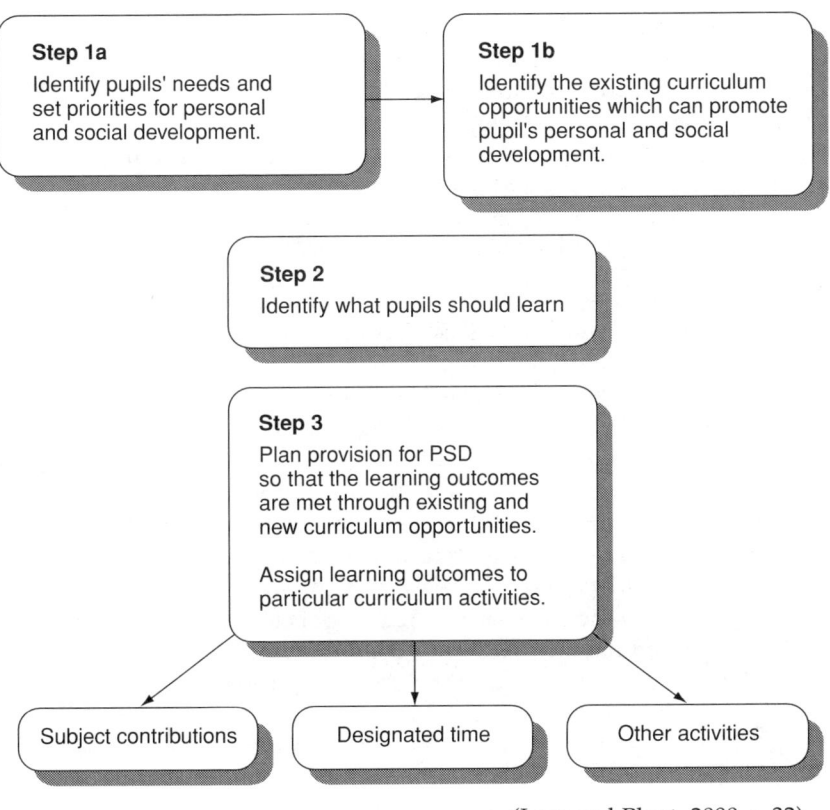

(Lees and Plant, 2000, p.32)

Similarly, the QCA's guidance for schools on 'planning for and implementing citizenship' clearly stresses the place of this in the arts, for instance recommending for Key Stages 3 and 4:

> *Aspects of the programmes of study for citizenship may be taught within and through other subjects, curriculum areas and GNVQ courses. Examples include: the role of the media in society and political and social issues found in English literature.... In addition to teaching some aspects of citizenship within other subjects, opportunities exist to make explicit links between aspects of citizenship and other aspects of the curriculum. Such links can be advantageous to both citizenship and the subject itself:*
>
> 1. Art and design: *issues of cultural diversity, their value and their expression;*
> 2. *Significance of the media;*
> 3. Music: *issues of cultural diversity, their value and their expression.*

(QCA, 2000, pp.13–14)

In planning the arts courses in a primary or secondary school there is huge scope for a variety of input, from the clearly PSD-focused to the brief allusion. The routes into PSD will be very varied, but most of them will give reciprocal support for the core arts courses.

The following list is a starting point of suggestions for ways to strengthen PSD in arts courses:

The lives of artists

How many pupils can go through three years of good arts teaching in a secondary school and learn about art but not learn about artists? Is it proper preparation for adult life? Is it right that we should never in three years of a lower school dwell for a moment on how artists spend their day or on the technicalities of working as an artist? It is true that we read the words on the page, see the picture in the frame, and hear the music in the instruments, and that our appreciative focus should indeed be on the work of art. But there will be times when the teacher can fit in biography – that much under used aspect of the full curriculum – modestly, effectively and relevantly into arts courses.

For instance, a dance teacher in a Year Eight class was using a number of different taped musical pieces for different variations of pupil choreography and dance. Before doing a technical study of contemporary/jazz style, derived from the work of Alvin Ailey, the teacher succinctly described his life and work, clearly related to the dance work of the pupils at that moment.

Such a vignette gives technical, community, and cultural input to the dance specialism, but it also touches on the relationship of human life and interests to work and the organisation of the arts.

At other times the biographical points may focus more on the artist's personal life, and thus support the theme of personal and social development.

There are many examples of artists who had dramatic events in their lives that in some way shaped their work, though it is important we do not inadvertently recreate the old notion that the creation of art *required* the stimulus of pain. Here are a few examples of twentieth-century artists whose work relates to their lives and to a considerable extent derives from aspects of stress or pain:

Freda Kahlo
1907–54; born Mexico, died Mexico
Kahlo began to paint while recovering in bed from a bus accident in 1925 that left her seriously injured. Her life's work of mostly self-portraits deals directly with her battle to survive. *Self-portrait* (1926, private collection), painted one year after her accident, shows a melancholy girl with long aristocratic hands and neck, depicted in a style with Latin-American sensibilities that reveals Kahlo's early love for Italian Renaissance art and especially for Botticelli.

Tracey Emin
1963–; born Britain
Emin's work is intimately autobiographical and often controversial; this artist's life is her most significant source material. Featured in the 1997 Royal Academy exhibition Sensation, *Everyone I have ever slept with 1963–1995* (1995, private collection) is an igloo-shaped tent embroidered and appliquéd with the names of everyone with whom she has shared a bed since birth (including her dying grandmother and her own aborted foetuses).

Oscar Kokoschka
1886–1980; born Vienna, died Britain
Kokoschka revolutionised the art of the turn of the twentieth century, adopting a radical approach to art, which was for him essential to the human condition and politically engaged. In 1934 he left Vienna after the establishment of an authoritarian corporate state, emigrating to London in 1938. His work at this time referred even more strongly to political events. The removal of his pictures from museums in Nazi Germany prompted him to paint *Self-portrait of a Degenerate Artist* (1937, private collection).

Chris Ofili
1968 –; born Britain
Ofili's work draws on popular culture and samples a wide range of cultural references in his work, famously incorporating elephant dung into his paintings. His head-on engagement with the stereotyping of black culture is comparable to the confrontational and inventive style of contemporary hip-hop music. In *No Woman, No Cry* (1998, Tate) Ofili intends the picture as a tribute to the murdered London teenager Stephen Lawrence, and to Lawrence's family who were subjected to intrusive media inquiry into the mishandling of the investigation by the Metropolitan Police. The title is drawn from the Bob Marley song of the same name.

Evelyn Glennie
Percussionist, composer
1966–; born Britain
This young Scotswoman has carved a new place for solo percussion in the realm of classical music, and has melded traditions and instrumentation from around the world. In the context of her career, the fact that Glennie has been profoundly deaf since the age of twelve seems amazing. But for her, it is virtually irrelevant. Hearing is basically a specialized form of touch and sound is simply vibrating air which the ear picks up. Glennie identifies the notes by the vibrations she feels through her feet and body.

A quick way into the lives of artists is to slip in a quotation. Here are a few examples of musicians' remarks (from Watson, 1991):

> *Courage is the mainspring of our best qualities; where it is lacking they wither, and without courage one is not even sufficiently prudent. One must, of course, consider, reflect, calculate, weigh the 'pros and cons'. But after that one must make up one's mind and act, without paying undue attention to the direction of the wind or to any passing clouds . . .*
>
> Franz Liszt (1811–86)
>
> Letter to Richard Pohl, 7 November 1868, quoted by Gal, *The Musician's World*

> *Only that art can live which is an active manifestation of the life of the people. It must be a necessary, and essential portion of that life, and not a luxury.*
>
> Ernst Bloch (1880–1959)
> Man and Music, 1917

> *An agreeable harmony for the honour of God and the permissable delights of the soul.*
>
> Johann Sebastian Bach (1685–1750)

> *Music – that wonderful universal language – should be a source of communication among men. Again I implore my fellow musicians throughout the world to put the purity of their art at the service of mankind in order to unite all races. Let each of us contribute as much as he can until this ideal is attained in all its glory.*
>
> Pablo Casals (1876–1973)

> *I will seize Fate by the throat; it shall certainly not bend and crush me completely.*
>
> Ludwig van Beethoven (1770–1827)
> Letter to F.G. Wegler, 1801

Which of the two powers, love or music, is able to lift man to the sublimest heights? It is a great question, but it seems to me that one might answer it thus: love cannot express the idea of music, while music may give and idea of love. Why separate the one from the other? They are the two wings of the soul.

Hector Berlioz (1803–69)
Memoirs

My own idea ... of which I have been fully conscious since I found myself as a composer – is the brotherhood of peoples, brotherhood despite all wars and conflicts. I try – to the best of my ability – to serve this idea in my music.

Béla Bartok (1881–1945)
Letter to Octavian Beu, 1931

One's work should be a salute to life.

Pablo Casals (1876–1973)

Thus in a variety of ways the people in the arts can contribute to the PSD elements in courses complementing the contribution of the works of art themselves. Many artists suffered personal grief and of course were less than perfect in all aspects of their lives. The exploration helps the pupils understand both the arts and human life.

Communication

One way in which the spoken arts of drama and performed readings help is by developing flexibility and range of vocal styles. It is important that certain texts are not kept away from pupils (as they sometimes have been) because 'our kids don't talk like that'. Learning lines from wide repertoire, from Ibsen to Brecht, Marlowe to Roald Dahl, encourages personal communication skills, and thus supports PSD if properly used.

Role play

In drama sessions, improvisation can be used to explore the personal and social effects of actions and ways of expressing one's self: 'If you were in that situation and a stranger came up to you and said this, how could you sensibly react?' Improvisation and role play should often be planned to serve the dramatic work in hand, but should also often be designed for personal and social growth.

Literature, including drama

Human relationships are the core of most literature. The narrative 'story' element and visual arts of portrayal both have a potential impact on the growing pupil's understanding of self and others.

Audience

Understanding how to be a member of an audience is crucial to the arts curriculum. Focusing on the human skills and approaches in the 'appreciation' of arts also strengthens PSD.

Rehearsing

A good question to consider from the PSD perspective is how a member of a cast or an instrumental ensemble can express honest criticisms or positive suggestions.

Conclusion

However the specific arts courses are patterned, the place of Personal and Social Development is very important and potentially major, with the reciprocal, complementary strength of the PSD deepening the understanding, enjoyment, and skill of the pupil in the arts, and the arts deepening and enriching their Personal and Social Development.

Technology

In some schools the visual and craft-focused arts are strongly part of the Design and Technology course, yet many people see technology as completely separated from art. Design and Technology emphasises 'design' in its broadest sense. In KS3 the programme of study requirements include eight aspects of 'developing, planning and communicating ideas', of which half are clearly aesthetic:
Pupils should be taught to:

- *respond to design briefs and produce their own design specification for products*
- *develop criteria for their designs . . .*
- *generate design proposals that match the criteria*
- *consider aesthetic and other issues that influence their planning . . .*

(DfEE and QCA, 1999, secondary, p.136)

'Design' is a wide concept, but it includes the aesthetic. Style, choice of materials, and even the choice of forms are not exclusively functional. It is helpful to ask questions about the materials used. What visual and tactile effect does the grain of wood have? How does the texture of different ceramic finishes alter the look, feel, and use of pottery?

Complementing those aspects by which 'art' supports 'technology design', the arts courses should teach far more consciously about their *use* of technology. In music, for instance, what does that term known by everyone as the name of a widely used instrument mean: 'piano'? It is short for 'pianoforte'. Why? What *technology* allowed the change from the harpsichord and clavichord to the 'pianoforte'? What about Brahms and the clarinet? Adolf Sax and the saxophones? The steel pan? The church organ? The Wurlitzer?

Both in music and drama there is the use of amplification, recording, broadcasting, and DVDs. How have the various revolutions in stage lighting, both lanterns and control panels, altered stage productions?

In graphic design how did moveable type alter the visual impact? What about linotype, and computerisation? Indeed, what about paper itself? How did technological changes affect the usability, cost, texture, and style of printing? What about the technology of the book? What were the major changes, and when, why, and how did they come about? Most pupils are taught about Caxton and moveable type, but the pagination and binding of a book is lost technological history.

Even the best arts courses in schools have tended to cut themselves off from a somewhat crude definition of 'technology'. In fact, courses in all the arts can cogently support the pupils' enquiring minds and understanding of technology in the world.

4 DELIVERY

The overall curriculum for any subject needs a planned range of routes and modes of delivery. This is clearly true of language (the 1975 *A Language for Life* philosophy has been renewed in QCA's National Literacy Strategy) and Personal and Social Education. It is particularly true of the arts, both because of their coverage of virtually 'the whole of life itself' and because of the place of audience in the arts. This chapter considers four aspects, and therefore relates to Sections 4 and 5 of Chapter 3.

4.1 The communal life of the school

How far does the curriculum stretch? Arts in schools have an established place beyond the 'subject' timetable. The curriculum includes the whole planned life of the school, not just the timetabled sessions between, say, 9am and 3.30pm. If there were a better phrase, we should ditch the words 'extra-curricular' because nothing that a teacher shows, says, or organises in a school should be *extra*-curricular, which means 'outside the curriculum'. It should all derive from the school-devised overall curriculum. So the teaching of arts should be all-embracing and complemented by a variety of activities beyond 'lessons'. Most of these ideally should be planned long-term, although serendipitous moments also have their value and should be deliberately made use of. Very often arts aspects can be reinforced by exploring the unexpected features of local, national, and even international life.

By the term 'communal life' we mean those experiences planned by the school primarily for the benefit of its pupils (though sometimes parents and local people might take part) that are not a specific part of a timetabled subject 'lesson' or tutorial session. Sometimes these experiences will be extensions of the work of a course department, for instance, an exhibition, a public performance, or an excursion. Other times they will be planned by middle or senior management for a section or the whole of the school.

We often underestimate how much is taught by a school's communal activities. Assemblies, special events, visitors, visits, special exhibitions, and ceremonies can all carry key artistic messages – and can 'deliver' parts of the arts curriculum. Most national discussion of education mentions only 'lessons' as classroom events. But pupils can learn from the whole variety of school communal life.

▆▆ The school environment

The school's built environment and its grounds are not only issues of practical use and health and safety, but also have a curriculum content: they teach in a variety of ways, especially the design and aesthetic faculties of the pupils.

The environment includes all those aspects that educate silently, stimulating or blunting according to their appearance. From the school noticeboard through its graphic design on letters and notices, lessons in looking, seeing, and appreciating are being given. Alas there are some schools in which 'teacher graffiti' is the dominant art form on display: notices such as 'Do not enter this room' in choice disarray.

Primary schools are often better than secondary for communal display. If the arts are valued, they should be on display in the public areas of the school, the functional notices and furniture should be pleasing, and the architecture and interior design visually interesting. It is also possible to have a constant sequence of adult artists' work, whether artefacts on display or pictured, reproductions of works of art, or pictures and posters about the performing arts.

Some schools have the benefit of 'built-in' art forms: statues, stained glass, wall carvings. Indeed, from the 1950s to 70s the Inner London Education Authority had a contractual agreement that a percentage of the building costs of every new school had to be devoted to an integral work of art. Some had fine stained glass (for example Abbey Wood) and others specially commissioned modern sculptures (for example Dalwood's *The Tree of Knowledge* at Rutherford School in Marylebone).

The detailing of woodwork, display frames, notices, and reception offices in the built environment has a key aesthetic aspect. Decorations – the style and the condition – speak of art. Sadly, well-designed architectural features are sometimes allowed to be marred or even lost. Instead they should be preserved and accentuated. All aspects of the school environment contribute to the arts curriculum. Even playground walls, entrance notices, and reception office windows have their aesthetic effect. The landscaping and planting certainly does. Henry Morris summed it up in the expansion of 'Village Colleges' in Cambridgeshire in the 1920s and 30s:

> 'Competent teachers and beautiful buildings are of equal importance; to this proposition I will admit no qualification whatever . . . it is the eternal lesson of Oxford and Cambridge. . . . Habituation is the golden method as old as Plato's republic. . . . The school, the technical college, the community centre which is not a work of art is . . . an educational failure.'

(Ree, 1995, p.100)

Assemblies

The sequence of assemblies is a key component of the 'corporate life' school. One secondary school used twenty-minute, communal, high-feature, presentation events to 'deliver' as vividly and as interestingly as possible an aspect of the whole-school curriculum, especially what is sometimes known as 'Personal-Social Education', and now re-stressed by QCA following the Crick report on 'Citizenship'. Similarly, assemblies can cover historical themes (for example the date of Kristallnacht, the centenary of a local building, an act of parliament), international events, scientific discoveries of the past, and so on. For instance, in February a school can hold an assembly to commemorate Bengali Language Martyrs' Day, a celebration of the Bengali language and literature.

Such assemblies can *use* art to illustrate a topic or *be about* an aspect of an art. Often a senior member of staff gives an oral presentation; pupils may participate in a quasi-performance; there may be visual or aural presentations; interesting visitors may speak or perform. These can be whole-school, for a key stage, or for one year. Aspects of the arts are especially successful, whether they are closely associated with an arts course, illustrate another course (for example a historical topic), or tackle a broader theme (for example spring).

The legal requirements for a 'collective act of worship', reiterated from the 1944 legislation in 1988, are more flexible than is generally recognised. Many Islamic, Anglican, and Catholic schools do weave an artistic theme into their genuinely religious assemblies. However, a secular school can focus communal assemblies on a wide variety of themes, including the arts. This is especially valuable in relating the art forms to social, personal, and emotional realms. If the parents of all the pupils opt their children out of collective acts of worship, the school does not have to hold them. It can then plan its range of assemblies to extend the whole school curriculum, both using the arts and supporting themes.

The following examples are of assemblies that included an aspect of the arts over a year in a central London school. Different genre, cultural traditions, and periods were included, sometimes as the sole form and sometimes as a supportive part. Some were Year Assemblies, and others Key Stage 3, Key Stage 4, or Sixth Form:

1. The architectural styles of both the interior and exterior of the school's campus were illustrated with student work.
2. Actors from the Central School of Speech and Drama performed two scenes from *Romeo and Juliet*.
3. Professor Keith Critchlow spoke on the history of Islamic art in relationship to the VITA (Visual Islamic Traditional Arts) degree show on loan to the school.
4. Bold Balladeers: shared Victorian history through Music Hall songs.
5. Slides of mother and child paintings were used to show the cultural and historical importance of motherhood – a response to students 'cursing' each others mothers.
6. Anup Kuma Biswas, Bangladeshi international cellist, played Vivaldi, Bach, and Brahms.
7. *'Danny Boy'*: History of the song included playing a traditional Irish version, Clapton's acoustic version, and showing elements used in recent recordings. The speakers looked at the meaning of the lyrics – in particular 'in sunshine and in shadow' and how the sense of loss is universal. The song could well apply to modern refugees' flight, as it was originally intended to underline the flight of the nineteenth-century Irish emigrant.
8. The built environment: A look at the diversity and richness of architectural styles around the school. This assembly was illustrated by artwork done on location by Key Stage 3 students.
9. A class from Year 9 presented a fashion show.
10. Ferdinand Dennis, distinguished Jamaican novelist and ex-pupil, spoke on his time in the school as a boy.
11. Hepburn: girl band with recent album was booked for a concert.
12. Year 9 class performed *Romeo and Juliet* interpretations.
13. 'Bacchus and Ariadne': Assembly was based on Titian's painting with reference to transcription work done by the students. Also involved retelling the tale of Ariadne and Theseus. (Other assemblies focussed on Picasso's *'Guernica'* and Gericault's *'Raft of Medusa'*.)

Special events

Many schools arrange special events for groups of classes on occasions when part of the course timetable is closed for the event or for an evening or weekend. The most common are prize events or leavers' farewells. Some schools have an annual prize day for the older students as a public ceremony featuring dance, drama, poetry, and music, thus using the arts to celebrate achievement.

More rarely but very valuably the arts are featured in combinations of exhibitions and performances to 'bring alive' some historical or social memory. Special dates commemorating events of history (especially local culture), international events, or famous people can bring aspects of the wide curriculum into a school event with an artistic core. For instance, 1996 was the centenary of William Morris' death, and the following is an external description of one school's special artistic/historical focus:

William Morris centenary celebration:
A school-based event bringing the arts together and relating them to social history.

What happened? This project was devised to celebrate the centenary of the death of William Morris, a man who had tried to break down the barriers between fine arts and crafts and promote the notion of arts for all. A cross-arts performance was the culmination of the project.

How did it come about? The school approached the education and audience development officer for the Orchestra of St John's, Smith Square, who had previously worked with the school. She arranged for the orchestra's composer in residence to work with staff and students. Their musical composition, poetry, and performance skills contributed to the event.

Who was it for? GCSE and A level music and drama students planned and performed for a general audience.

What was the point? One of the principal aims was to celebrate the actual centenary day of Morris' death. The Headteacher was keen to demonstrate *'the complementary interconnection of the arts — the inter-relationship between the arts and life — social history in particular'*. He thought that because Morris believed that the arts were not only for a limited range of people he was particularly relevant to students in his multicultural inner-city school. The orchestra's general aims for their educational work are similarly to encourage everyone to use their own creativity and to increase appreciation and enjoyment of the arts, whilst making them more accessible.

What did they look at? To illustrate another aspect of Morris' work, an exhibition of his wallpaper and fabrics and early editions of his books were displayed in an exhibition area of the school foyer. The material was loaned to the school by an antiquarian bookseller.

How did they prepare? Students' awareness of William Morris as a polymath was raised at an introductory weekend course which included talks and the performance of a play written by the head of drama and performed by the drama students.

What did the students do? GCSE music students worked with the composer in residence to create a string quartet, based on a study of the text of a William Morris poem. A master class was arranged with a cellist from the orchestra and workshops for the school's string players were held. The head of drama worked with ten GCSE drama students to compile the spoken presentations for the concert. They first discussed his conviction about the right of all people to have access to education and the arts. Unexpectedly, Morris' socialist beliefs were of great interest to the students.

What did the students learn? The musical scores far exceeded expectations and demonstrated the value of working with professional musicians. Each student's composition was taped for their GCSE coursework. The composer in residence felt that students had understood the difference in sequencing and composing and that working with professional instrumentalists helped them to *'see the difference between a good idea and a bad one'*.

Drama students studied Morris' love poems and, despite the complex symbolism, enjoyed them. They discovered that the performance of poetry was very different from studying it in an English lesson.

Students became aware of Morris as an artist, designer, architect, socialist, writer, poet and teacher. They were fascinated by this since, in school, these skills are separated into different subject compartments. They thought that Morris' style, which they learned is still popular today, was old-fashioned although they were excited by his political stance.

Ideas for taking the project further
The head of drama felt that her students had become very involved in the project and that ideas and concepts gained from it could be discerned in later GCSE course work. Music students' experience led to further original composition.

The performance included all the above as well as a slide sequence of Morris' designs with commentary, and a brief talk on his place in history.

(Wilkinson & Clive, 2001, pp.89–92)

What we have called 'special events' feature in a number of schools, but not as often as would be desirable. Whilst they will not always have the desired impact, they are a significant way of encouraging a real and continuing excitement about the arts. David Hargreaves undertook an important piece of arts research into this subject. He interviewed a large number of adults who came from working-class backgrounds and had come to love the performing arts. He then analysed that set of memories, and demonstrated that their enthusiasm was not based on incremental tuition, but came from the impact of a powerful experience:

> *One of the most immediate and striking features of my informants' accounts of how they came to be interested in an art form is the frequency with which they cite a particular event or experience . . . Some describe the experience as 'shattering'. It did indeed cause a kind of wound, one which injured or destroyed all their preconceptions about the art form, to which hitherto they were often hostile or indifferent. . . . preconceptions are destroyed by an unexpectedly pleasant experience.*
>
> (Hargreaves, 1983, p.140)

The suggestion, then, is that many or even most young people who are excited by the performing arts are first turned on by an intense experience. The problem is that it is difficult to plan for such excitement in the curriculum. The events are likely to require unusual contexts. To create occasions like that must tax the routine planning of a school; however, it should be attempted.

Exhibitions

Opportunities for simply looking at pictures and talking about them are rarer than they should be for children of all ages. The author of a book of good quality reproductions of beautiful and interesting pictures for younger children wrote:

> *You do not need to be a teacher or an art historian to share a painting with a child. Children love exploring pictures and finding in them familiar and unfamiliar things. . . . By opening our children's eyes to art, we can help them to understand the world in which they live and the people with whom they share it.*
>
> (Micklethwait, 1996, p.9)

One term a school had an exhibition of Indian miniature art in Mogul tradition, a tradition that goes back a couple of hundred years. There was no 'teaching' given about the exhibition – the pictures were simply hung. A day would not go past when there would not be somebody just standing and looking and saying: 'Gosh!' That kind of permeation of the school, in the planned and unplanned encounters and occasions, events and displays, is part of a whole-school arts curriculum.

Art exhibitions by local artists, students, and visiting professionals can take place regularly. Often national organisations or commercial firms offer travelling exhibitions. Theatres in the wide geographical area of a school will often be willing regularly to send posters, programmes, and photographic displays.

Local artists' work should be displayed and purchased; local galleries advertised and visited; local industry persuaded to sponsor; local minority ethnic groups' art traditions featured; and the art of local religious groups explored. There are excellent photographers in most areas who are pleased to have their work displayed. The artistic life of the school should interact with the 'communities' of the neighbourhood. These should not be seen too rigidly as 'geographical': these are also commercial, occupational, religious, cultural, and specific-interest communities.

Clearly exhibitions require display facilities (discussed in Chapter 5, Section 2) and technical-administrative staff (discussed in Chapter 5, Section 3). It would also help if there were more local and national organisations providing touring displays. (A sample of those currently so doing is listed in the Appendix.) Since 1991 Sainsbury's has had a national scheme 'to expose young people to art in their general environment' by donating framed reproductions. A few Local Education Authorities have loan schemes.

The most important requirement of a school in this context is inventiveness and flexibility, supported by ingenious administrators who can make the contacts and raise the funding. The following examples of actual in-school exhibitions are a small selection of the infinite possibilities:

1. A range of photographs of a performance of a play

2. Photographs to chart the migration and settlement of Bangladeshis in Britain

3. Posters of an era or of a particular product over the years

4. Ephemera from the Second World War evacuation

5. Ceramics from a local pottery

6. The recent work of local artists

7. Photographs of local buildings

8. A 'pictorial biography' of eminent artists

9. Medieval Christian art reproductions

10. Islamic design
11. Pictures of dance
12. Rabindranath Tagore's paintings in reproduction to support the study of his poetry
13. Nineteenth-century wrought and cast iron
14. Textiles in an Asian traditional style
15. Chinese woodblock prints.

Finally, it is also good to have some pictures and artefacts on permanent display, with appropriate captions. Pupils who 'grow up' with a picture see it afresh as they mature – especially if there are references (not too often) in assemblies and lessons.

The public-address system and publications

A whole-community approach weaves the curriculum into almost every aspect of the school lives of the pupils, sometimes specifically but very often as an almost subliminal theme.

Most secondary schools use a public-address system for a coordinating member of the senior management team to speak to the whole school (pupils and staff) at the start and end of the day, and often at other times as well. Whilst there are some schools where these 'announcements' sound impersonal and distanced, most schools endeavour to convey their ethos, in both style and content.

It is possible to mention external artistic news, such as local or national events, and refer to anniversaries and famous artists. If the sound input equipment has been adequately adapted, it can broadcast excerpts from recordings, including recitation of poetry and drama interviews, and commentaries. Carefully selected musical excerpts are also very effective, whether a wartime song to mark a twentieth-century war date or an eighteenth-century instrumental fragment to evoke a moment in history of that period. A recorded voice, perhaps from the British Library's 'National Sound Archive', can speak of an artistic experience. These sound inputs help include the wider arts curriculum in the communal life of the school.

Finally, the communal life includes all school publications. Programmes for exhibitions, concerts, and performances are obvious, although their content, illustrations, and graphic design should be beautiful as well as functional. When the internationally famous opera singer, Jessye Norman, opened the new Studio Theatre at North

Westminster Community School in the 1980s, the printed programme was a small but meaningful part of the artistic content of the evening. Similarly, one school's annual literary prize ensured that the booklet of the short-listed pupil-writers' short-stories was a pleasing piece of design. The judge, an eminent writer, was fully evoked biographically, thus carrying arts curriculum content. Publicity booklets, school induction booklets, and Key Stage 4 option prospectuses can be aesthetically satisfying and also carry artistic messages.

Conclusion

Ingenuity, good organisation, co-operation, careful planning, and modest financial resources can ensure that the communal life of the school enriches the arts curriculum, giving it breadth, variety, contextual differentiation, and a strong social-experiential impact.

4.2 The use of public arts

The fundamental purpose of access policy and practice is to ensure that everyone can physically use a building, reach the artwork or production on offer, and be helped towards an understanding and enjoyment of it to the extent that they need or want. No-one should be excluded, deliberately or unintentionally, because of physical, social, educational or cultural barriers.

Within an arts venue or organisation, there can be institutional, professional, personal, social, or environmental barriers to access and inclusion, or barriers related to internal perceptions and awareness. More basic barriers include policies on charging and opening hours.

Peer-group attitudes and the influences of parents and teachers were described in the Calouste Gulbenkian report on extending young people's access to cultural venues as a 'mixture of psychological and physical factors [making] the development of strategies for increasing access a complex task' (*Crossing the Line*, Harland and Kinder, 1999).

What has all this to do with schools? One of the main difficulties in ensuring access (in all its forms) is a lack of collaboration between arts venues or companies and the young people and teachers they seek to attract. Teachers and their students can work together and then engage with the venues to devise suitable programmes and ways of delivering those programmes, which are mutually beneficial. This avoids the situation of venues saying: this is what we offer; take it or leave it. It is not good enough if teachers and young people come away disappointed or, worse, untouched by the experience. The success of those many programmes and projects that do meet schools' needs make it imperative that all such schemes 'work'.

The *Crossing the Line* report helps with this task by asking some pertinent questions about access and young people. For example:

1. How can venues interact with the culture of young people and develop links with them, while retaining their commitment to their more traditional audiences?
2. How can cultural venues become more inviting to young people?
3. How can the arts in cultural venues be made more familiar and relevant to young people?
4. How can young people contribute to the programming process?
5. How can the work of venues be made more relevant to non-western cultures?
6. What role does new technology play in attracting, maintaining and developing young people as audiences?
7. What is the value and role of special schemes and initiatives; how can their momentum be sustained; and how do they fit into the main work of venues and schools, and into regional and government priorities?
8. What specific training and skills are needed to promote greater access and to handle the issues raised above?
9. How can the work be monitored and evaluated effectively; what can be termed 'success'; and how might that be built on?

Access is used in terms of an organisation opening itself up, and of potential audiences or visitors taking up what is on offer, both as viewers and as participants. An organisation must not just make itself accessible, but must also take steps to encourage people in.

The Creative Partnerships programme currently being developed by the DCMS through the Arts Council of England aims to ensure that young people 'will be able to access a wide range of activities, events, and opportunities across the creative sector' plus having the visionary leadership to 'mobilise collaborations and opportunities for, with and on behalf of young people'.

Creative Partnerships have been set up in sixteen locations across the country to bring together schools, arts and other creative organisations, including commercial creative industries, to provide enhanced opportunities for every child in the area. For more information, see the Arts Council website: artscouncil.org.uk.

This is an opportunity for successful ways of improving access to be replicated and refined elsewhere and for more schools to be part of such schemes. For example, here are some of the visual arts initiatives featured in the *Crossing the Line* report:

- A major art gallery set up an advisory group of people aged between fourteen and 25 who worked with gallery staff on a programme of activities for their peers. This consultation over an extended period played a vital role in enabling the gallery to fine-tune its services for young people.

- A Test Drive the Arts scheme encouraged young Asians to visit a range of mainstream arts venues. Ten young Asians were recruited via focus groups to act as 'arts ambassadors' with each recruiting a further ten young Asians among their friends and colleagues.

- A new art gallery consulted local people, including young people, about the design of the new building, the look of publicity material, the atmosphere of the foyer and the cafe. Entrance to the gallery is free. The report concluded:

[Young people's] sensitivity to the ambience of the gallery environment, and the welcome it implied, highlights a comprehensive interpretation of access, which cultural venues may need to embrace if they wish to encourage young people to be regular visitors.

- Among a range of projects to attract young people as 'critical spectators' rather than through direct 'hands-on' activities, one gallery explored art, design and architecture through interpretation. Another recruited young people through youth clubs and used exhibitions to enable them to work out their own approach to interpretation and reflect on their preferences.

Participants felt confident in their ability to form their own opinions and wanted more interactive interpretation, as well as a more interactive experience within the gallery as a whole.

The arts are increasingly being seen as a key element in promoting social inclusion. In 1997, Comedia published the results of a study into the social impact of arts programmes (Matarasso, 1997). It found that participation in the arts:

1. is an effective route to personal growth, leading to enhanced confidence, skill-building and educational developments which can improve people's social contacts and employability;

2. contributes to social cohesion by developing networks and understanding, and building local capacity for organisation and self-determination;

3. brings benefits in other areas such as environmental renewal, health promotion, and creativity in organisational planning;

4. produces visible social change that can be evaluated and planned;

5. represents a flexible, responsive, and cost-effective part of a community development strategy;

6. strengthens Britain's cultural life and forms a vital factor of success in social policy.

In effect, the arts have a substantial part to play in addressing current social challenges. Their creativity, openness and elasticity are at the heart of that social impact. The Comedia report concludes that a marginal adjustment of priorities in cultural and social policy can deliver real socio-economic benefits. It recommends a framework for developing participatory arts initiatives in public policy, based on seven core principles: clear objectives, equitable partnership, good planning, shared ethical principles, excellence, proportional expectations, and joint evaluation.

These conclusions are influencing government policy, and showing schools and arts organisations what they might be capable of in terms of using the arts to enhance the lives of children and young people and their communities. For example, the arts can be a vital part of school and local education authority (LEA) development plans, and of such initiatives as Excellence in Cities.

Significantly, the arts are now a key element in government strategies for building social inclusion, which in turn often depends on educational initiatives. In July 1999, the DCMS policy action team reported to the Government's Social Exclusion Unit on the role of arts, sport and leisure in regenerating poor neighbourhoods.

The report *Arts and Sport*, (DCMS, 1999) concluded that these activities contribute to neighbourhood renewal and 'make a real difference' to education (as well as health, crime and employment) in deprived communities. It recommended that:

1. the DfEE (now the DfES) encourage schools to use creative activity to support the drive to raise literacy and numeracy standards, and

to build pupils' confidence and self-esteem through personal, social and health education (PSHE);

2. local authorities make the widest feasible use of school arts facilities out of school hours.

The DCMS has now issued its long-term plan *Culture and Creativity: The next ten years* (March 2001). This distils its approach to education, social inclusion and access, although much of it relies on action by the DfES (some of which was simultaneously promised in the white paper *Schools: Achieving success*). This DCMS plan includes the 'cultural pledge . . . that, in time, every pupil will have the chance to work with creative professionals and organisations, and thereby to enrich their learning across the whole curriculum'. This, of course, will depend on the success of the Creative Partnerships project (see above). But it encourages all schools to start now to build effective and rewarding collaborations with the arts beyond the school.

Other proposals include the right for every child at primary school to have the opportunity (should they want it) to learn a musical instrument; the opportunity to learn the ICT expertise that will underpin the creative skills of the future; the increase of specialist teachers in the arts for schools in deprived areas; and a greater premium on creativity and cultural appreciation in the curriculum for initial teacher training.

This ten-year plan has, in part, grown out of the DCMS's *New Cultural Framework* policy, which set up strategic regional bodies for all cultural interests and key agencies, and requires local authorities to devise local cultural strategies (currently being piloted in a sample of authorities). It involves four basic aims:

1. promoting access for the many, not just the few;

2. pursuing excellence and innovation;

3. nurturing educational opportunity; and

4. fostering the creative industries.

These developments should, if pursued with determination and resources, make for a stronger presence for cultural activities, greater access to funding sources, and more effective support mechanisms for schools. One key point is that arts education can be provided and funded from a wider range of agencies and initiatives, as much social as educational or cultural, as much commercial as public sector.

4.3 Devising the specific arts courses

As we stressed in Chapter 1, Section 3, and Chapter 3, Section 3, one of the most difficult curriculum-planning decisions after the overall, whole-school content has been detailed is to define the *courses* through which that content will be put across to the pupils. *'Subject'* now (post 1988 legislation) is best thought of as an analytic, *planning* content, and *'course'*, we suggest, as the technical title for the separately taught activity on the timetable. Significantly, a course can be continuous throughout the year or across the years, or for only a part of the year in a rotation. This is often helpfully known as a 'modular course'. Further, a course can have sub-courses, such as a 'languages' course having a term of Spanish, a term of German, and a term of French.

In the arts there has always been considerable argument about when to combine and when to specialise. As we detail in Chapter 1, Section 3, the 'subject' nomenclature and content divisions of the National Curriculum are central government *planning* divisions. They do not have to be co-terminus with the courses in a school, nor does that terminology have to be used for the courses. A school really can define as it chooses any 'courses' by title and content, providing the National Curriculum content is somewhere included, whether mixed into different courses, isolated into one, or combined. For instance, Ofsted inspection has confirmed that a Key Stage 3 'Humanities' course weaving together History, Religious Education, and Geography is fully legal.

This flexibility was spelt out at the time of the 'National Curriculum' introduction in the *Education Reform Act 1988*, as we argued in detail in Chapter 1, Section 3. One sentence in the DES notes to the House of Commons, when the Act was a Bill before the House, made this absolutely clear:

> There is no requirement that the school timetable should be organised so as to include separate lessons in each foundation subject; nor any requirement as to the amount of time which should be spent on each.

Thus, *any* combination of the requirements for 'art', 'music', 'English' (e.g. 'literature', 'moving image', 'media', 'drama'), 'Design Technology', 'Information and Communication Technology', and 'Dance activities' (listed in 'Physical Education') from the National Curriculum (DfEE and QCA, 1999) together with *any* other aspect of the arts a school wishes to include is *fully* legal.

The overall 'Faculty' or 'Subject Department' could be grouped as 'Combined Arts', 'Technology and Art', 'Expressive Arts', or as single arts. In many schools 'drama' and 'media' are taught in 'English'. Indeed the Qualifications and Curriculum Authority texts place them under that subject heading.

Examples of actual courses

Course Title	Arts Included
English	drama, literature, and media
Performing Arts	dance, drama, film, music
Dance and Drama	dance and drama
Expressive Arts	art, drama, music
Physical Education	dance
Design Technology and Arts	D & T, art, music, textiles
Home Economics	textiles

The different arts can be taught by different specialists in what could be thought of as 'grouped' modular sub-courses. For instance, in 'Performing Arts' or 'Arts and Design Technology', the different, component arts are usually taught by different specialists. Sometimes these grouped courses are open to criticism that the individual arts are taught too separately, without the interactions being adequately highlighted. For instance, dance has a substantial element relating to drama and another substantial element relating to music. There are advantages in considering 'the arts' as a whole, and a number of the arts specialisms benefit from being studied together. Indeed, each is capable of providing insight into the others.

However, the inclusion of an art in other courses can suffer from the opposite effect – the main content of the course eroding and limiting the artistic depth of the art. This needs particular consideration for 'Drama' in an 'English' course and 'Dance' in 'Physical Education'. Whilst there is much excellent drama in English courses and drama of course links closely with literature and media, studies suggest that the essence of drama, its theatricality, and its relationship to dance and music is harder to achieve in an 'English' course. 'Dance' in 'Physical Education' (discussed in Chapter 3, Section 3) can work well when the teacher is a true specialist. However, studies have shown that the dance element in a PE teacher's training is usually very slight. Further, the interactive relationship between the cultural range of dance and the media aspects of sports and gymnastics is minimal. A postal survey of teachers in 1988 showed 5% recommending dance as 'a free-standing subject on its own'; 32% 'as part of PE and Games'; and 63% 'as part of a Performing Arts Department'.

4.4 Presenting the art work of pupils

Most schools display pupils' artwork and some have readings of pupils' literature. Almost all have dramatic and musical performances by pupils (sometimes of work of their own creation), and a much smaller group have pupil dance performances. However, comparatively few secondary schools weave pupils' artistic work into the communal life of the school with a comprehensively planned range of presentations – performances, competitions, and displays.

Exhibitions of visual arts

Most schools work hard and skilfully to mount exhibitions of pupils' work. Some do not manage this as effectively as a full consideration of the overall arts curriculum would require. For instance, exhibitions should cover the full range of pupil arts – not only the visual arts of painting and drawing, but also photographs of built artefacts, dance, drama, ceramics and built three-dimensional objects, graphics, and typography.

An example of the linking of creativity, historic learning about art, and public display was a beautiful exhibition of paintings by around twenty Year 7 to 11 pupils at Highbury Grove School in London under the thematic title *'Influences'*. The explanatory caption explained the exhibition of vivid illustrations (box opposite).

The practical and imaginative school will truly *use* its full range of display possibilities as part of the delivery of the arts curriculum.

We strongly recommend that pupils' visual arts are displayed as often as possible with the full skill of a professional art gallery, just as pupils' literature should sometime be printed with the professional care of copy-editing, graphic design, and good reproduction. Visual arts are often well displayed in the working environment of the art-teaching rooms – normally on pinboard. Of course, pinboard is quick to use and offers a large space so that many pupils' work can be shown simultaneously. However, it denies the pupil the visual impact and symbolic gesture of the frame. Specially made frames with easily removable backs or even Velcro backing for the easy fixing of pictures can be very useful: there should be occasions when a picture by a pupil is given that focus and displayed in a public part of the school.

The Institution of Civil Engineers has each year organised a national competition for paintings by pupils aged five to seven showing an aspect of the contributions of engineering to human life. Apart from the

> **INFLUENCE :-** n. l) (usually followed by *on*) effect a person or thing has on another.
>
> Throughout history artists examining the world around them have been influenced by the work of other artists and the art of other cultures. This has been a fertile and productive area for many artists. Numerous examples of this exist: Picasso and 'Cubism' was influenced by African art; Andy Warhol was influenced by the mass commercial and throw-away culture of sixties America.
>
> At Highbury Grove we try and encourage our students to look, examine and explore the world around them as well as the work of a variety of different artists. The artwork on display here represents just such a view.
>
> The influences represented here include modern Japanese Comic book art, in particular MANGA, African art, Indian, Chinese and Celtic art.
>
> The artwork presented here is from a range of different year groups, from Year 7 to the Sixth Form. Each contribution shows how a student has developed her or his own individual view in relation to a contextual influence.
>
> **REMEMBER .... BY LOOKING AT THESE PICTURES YOU ARE ALSO BEING INFLUENCED**
>
> (Murray Aikman – Highbury Grove School, 2001)

major prizes, the long-listed competitors had their pictures framed – and this really excited the pupils and pleased parents and schools.

If possible, often have an art exhibition in the school. Pupils should not have art only to look at in a lesson: it should be on the public walls. And never mind if some of them have not looked at it. Some of them will, and some of them who say they have not looked at it will actually have seen something all the same. Similarly, there need to be publications; there also need to be events, such as a launch by a distinguished person of an exhibition of pupils' work.

Literature

Whilst the most important feedback to pupils on their writing is that of the pupils' particular teacher, and whilst the reading aloud in classrooms by pupils or teachers and informal displays in those classrooms are all crucial, these activities should be complemented by occasional, more formal presentations. After all, adult, professional writers benefit from formal review, performances, and publishing.

(a) Publication
Adult writers have their work copy-edited so it comes back to them with the polishing skills of a professional. It is then printed so that reading the work is both easier and more pleasurable, and can reach many more readers. This is quite different from the pinned-up hand-written and corrected pupil original. 'Copy-editing' is a skill rarely described in English lessons. Pupil writers often learn from having their work copy-edited, word processed, and replicated on a well laid-out page.

The life of the school is also enhanced if at least occasionally pupils' writing can be published, and copies available widely. Thus, once a year in one London secondary school six short stories from each of the three sections of the school are printed. They are copy-edited and the booklets are designed by a good graphic designer, so they come back in the way that an adult writer's would. This encourages those writers and others, and contributes to the communal artistic and intellectual life of the school.

(b) Performances
Many schools include readings of pupils' poetry, prose, and sometimes drama, for instance in assemblies. Often this is by the writer, another pupil, or a member of staff. Such 'performances' are very valuable. It is, though, worth considering occasional more 'formal' performances, such as:

1. pupils being 'produced' by one of the school's drama specialists to give a polished performance;
2. a visiting experienced professional reader performing a selection of items;
3. an extract from a play written by a pupil directed for staging as part of a ceremony such as a Prize Evening;
4. a poem broadcast from a rehearsed, pre-recorded reading over the school's PA.

▬ Ceramics, wood-carving, and sculpture

There is considerably less 3D art than is ideal because of the technical problems, though a number of schools do have a strong place for ceramics. Where pupils can work on these three-dimensional forms, it is valuable if the work can be skilfully photographed for inclusion in school and other local publications. Good display facilities should be well illuminated and secure.

Music

Most schools arrange a variety of opportunities for pupils to perform for other pupils, parents, and visitors, although nationally the proportion of pupils playing an instrument or singing is fairly low. How can a school best organise performing opportunities, if the school has the appropriate spaces, equipment, and administrative support?

The ideal criteria would include:

1. a range from the most casual: 'let's listen to Maya and Hamish play their duet', to major, formally presented performances that have been widely advertised

2. some opportunities to perform on the same platform and occasionally in the same group as adult performers, including professional ones

3. a variety of musical styles and periods.

The 'School Concert' remains a very valuable and by no means a dated activity. Ideally this should be complemented by musical items inserted into many other events. Sometimes they would be purely 'music' slots but on other occasions inserted to illustrate a theme. For instance, in one London school a presentation of the history of the area had a late nineteenth-century popular song played and danced by pupils. An evening of the work of Rabindranath Tagore had a composition by a pupil inspired by one of Tagore's poems, played by pupil instrumentalists. A history of the early nineteenth century 'Ragged Schools' had a song written for them (quoted on page 110) sung and accompanied by pupils. Performances should be organised to illustrate and support events related to different cultures, different periods of history, and different famous dates.

Finally, there is the place of recording. A number of schools have produced CDs. For instance, Forest School, an independent school in Snaresbrook, put together six years of recordings to produce a CD for pupils, parents, staff, and friends of the school:

> *After many years of collecting recordings, we have just had our first CD mastered and printed. Entitled* Archive Recordings *it features outstanding performances from Forest's choirs, bands, orchestra and soloists from the last six years. Priced at a mere £5, all monies raised from sales will be divided approximately half and half between the CD costs and our local charity, Haven House.*
>
> *At such a price the CD makes an excellent present for friends and relations. It includes an enormous variety of music with such groups as the Chapel Choir,*

Friday Choir, Lower School Girls' Choir, Forest Swingers, Big Band, Jazz Band, Blues Band, Chamber Orchestra, String Chamber Ensemble, 76 string players from this year's String Prom and various soloists.

The pupils' musical performing can be woven into the work of the school in a variety of ways, sometimes with major emphasis and on other occasions just as background. This range and combination benefits all aspects of the arts curriculum.

Drama and dance

As 'performing' arts there is, of course, a substantial tradition of the presenting of pupils' work, especially of drama. The proportion of schools teaching dance, however, is rather low and the ones within that number which give fully staged dance performances even fewer. Both arts, however, benefit from presentations to audiences, sometimes fairly informally, but also in proper, fully *staged* performances. There was a time when a number of drama education specialists were critical of school drama being too closely linked to stage performances with scenery, lighting, and sound. 'Education drama' was private and better without such formalities, they sometimes argued. In this century we can surely maintain a balance, and relish the full staging of performances for almost all ages of children. Indeed, the effect, for instance, of properly designed and operated stage lighting is a major contribution to the performers' grasp of drama as well as increasing the impact on the members of the audience.

Of course, many schools do not have fully fitted theatre-type halls. However, many school halls, including those in primary schools, become virtual theatres if fitted with a stage lighting system. Those very few that have dedicated theatres (for example Forest School, North Westminster Community School, Christ's Hospital School) have an immense advantage for this aspect of presenting pupils' artistic work. However, a typical school hall can also be very effective if well fitted, and modern electronic switchboards wired to overhead, internally wired lighting barrels with truly efficient blackout can make the hall into an effective theatre.

Conclusion

The coherent school will have a complementary and interactive approach to building opportunities for the young person to be both creative artist and responsive audience – the two mutually supportive roles.

5 SUPPORTING THE DELIVERY

Most teachers express the need for more significant, more focused, and more tangible 'support'. Those working in the arts in schools have often had very strong and warm encouragement, but may also have struggled against problems. These include overall 'curriculum' planning (which we have covered in Chapter 3), which sometimes lacked a comprehensive and fully artistic vision of the place of arts in the whole-school curriculum. Very important, though, is the range of support resources.

Every aspect of schooling requires adequate resourcing in terms of teachers, support staff, accommodation, equipment, learning materials, and consumables. It also requires full understanding from the schools' overall staffing and administrative structure. However, even where the vision of the arts has been present, in too many schools there has been inadequate funding. The LEA, governors, senior management, and specialist arts staff should consider in their arts reviews and policy development the range of support in terms of funding, accommodation, facilities and equipment, support staff and partnership possibilities.

5.1 Funding and resourcing

What is sufficient for the arts? And how much is likely to be coming your way, irrespective of your needs? Monitoring on a national basis what the arts in school receive from delegated budgets has been a rare event. When figures have been published, they seem more a rule of thumb than offering real insight into the resources available. What is clear, though, is that the figures involved are meagre.

For 1995/96 Ofsted reported that annual spending on art in secondary schools ranged from 'the very poor' at 70p per pupil to 'very good' at more than £8 (Dudley LEA and AAIAD, 1996). The median value was £2.88, unchanged from the previous year. At the time, Ofsted commented:

Some schools have only just enough resources to sustain the range, type and scale of work that National Curriculum and examination courses demand.

Ofsted has never repeated this exercise in England. However, in 1999, the Welsh schools inspectorate published *Art, Drama and Music in Key Stages 3 and 4* (SPAEM/OHMCI, 1999), a report on inspections of arts subjects in secondary schools. It indicated that the range of spending per pupil was even lower:

- art from under £1 to £5;
- music from under £1 to over £3;
- drama up to a maximum of £1.50, when not subsumed into the allocation for English or Welsh.

The inspectorate commented:

Where the allocations are in the lower part of the range, this can have an inhibiting effect on the quality of pupils' work and pupils either have to purchase their own materials, or make do with a limited range and quantity.

In 2001, a survey, carried out by Artworks (the National Children's Art Awards) with the support of NSEAD (the National Society for Education in Art and Design), and AAIAD (the Association for Advisers and Inspectors for Art and Design), revealed the following:

In secondary schools:

The average annual spend on consumable materials through capitation is just £2.68 per pupil. Some schools spend as little as 60p a year on each pupil. The maximum being spent is £7.30.

Even in specialist schools, the average annual spend per pupil is £3.08, with a range of 61p up to a maximum of £5.34. Scottish secondary schools fare better than English and Welsh ones, with an average spend of £3.75 per pupil per year.

The difference in textbook spending between independent schools and state schools has been widely publicised. It is less well known that independent schools in England and Wales spend almost five times more than state schools on consumable materials in the arts. The average annual spend per pupil in the independent sector is £12.40, with a minimum of £2.00 and a maximum of £26.68. This difference is accentuated when comparing the annual amount spent on those pupils taking art and design (an exercise not carried out by Ofsted). In state schools, the average annual spend is £4.87 (and £4.27 in specialist schools), but in independent schools it is £28.38.

Only a third of state secondary schools report that they receive any additional funding for art and design resources on top of normal capitation. Those that do, tend to rely on small and variable amounts rather than regular sources of funding. The average annual amount in additional income is just £366.32. Specialist schools are better off with an average of £1,449.

The most common sources are income from taking on initial teacher training students, and successful bids for extra funds from within the school allocated by the headteacher or the parent-teacher association. Larger sums of money are also obtained from a variety of sources by some schools for new equipment or curriculum development. Where schools do lack funds, some ask Key Stage 4 pupils to buy their own equipment. Other schools run art shops on a commercial basis, although more schools go for a not-for-profit venture.

In primary schools:

It is difficult to assess accurately how much is spent on consumable materials for art and design in primary schools because money is spent via individual class budgets. Some schools estimate that on average around 40% of their consumable materials budget goes to art and design. This suggests that primary schools' average annual spend per pupil on art and design consumables is £1.18 at Key Stage 1 and £1.29 at Key Stage 2.

Just under a third of schools (30%) report that the amount they spend annually on art and design materials is increasing; but 15% (one school in seven) says the amount is falling. The rest (55%) report that it is staying the same.

Primary schools spend most money on paper, card, and paints; followed by drawing materials, clay, and pastels. The expensive items include clay, card, textiles, 3D materials, and good-quality brushes and paints. But as one teacher comments: 'The little things add up – glue, paper, pencils.'

Many schools depend on seeking out or being given free materials, and most will accept anything on offer in order to resource particular specialisms. However, this takes time that needs to be built into teachers' schedules. Alternatively, governors and parents can be recruited to do this, because their own interests or jobs give them access to certain items or materials. Some schools run competitions or put on arts events to attract sponsorship, and sell the products from children's arts lessons or projects.

All the figures quoted above must be regarded as impracticable – too small with which to run an effective and wide-ranging programme in any of the main art forms, let alone those schools which seek to offer a broader range of art form options. What is surprising is that many schools do manage, or at least survive.

It should not, and does not, have to be like that. Provision for the arts in school needs to be underpinned by access to sufficient resources, in terms of people and their expertise, of equipment and structures that suit the art form, and of money to pay for them and for a range of activities that can embrace pupils' diverse interests.

Ensuring sufficiency

All subject areas have to compete for the limited resources available to schools. The first task for arts staff is to ensure that the arts are competing on equal terms with those other subject areas. This is not to argue that every subject should get the same. Some, by their nature, inevitably require more resources. What the arts teacher should be after is sufficiency rather than sameness.

The first task is to assess how much each art form has:

- What is spent now?
- Where are the gaps?
- What can we not do because of lack of resources?

And what each art form needs:

- What is sufficient?
- What is needed to innovate or explore new directions?

A map of the economy

This is where a financial mapping of arts provision can be useful. Set out to find answers to:

- What financial resources are available now within the school for the arts generally and for each art form?
- What financial resources are used from outside the school?
- How are they currently used?
- What non-arts sources of funding are potentially accessible to the arts?

You also need to ask how well the school is performing financially:

- Is spending on the arts on track and under control?
- Are we getting value for money?

Of course, there are wider aspects to the resources available that have to be built into any such exercise in order to reach a clear understanding of the current situation and potential of the school's arts provision. For example:

1. What is the condition of the equipment and premises used by the arts?
2. What is the range and depth of expertise of the arts staff, individually and collectively?
3. What is the level and range of external support for the arts on which the school can draw?

The answers to all the above questions should give you a detailed picture of spending on the arts in the school. This can provide you with a foundation on which to:

1. build an effective case to negotiate basic and additional funding and other resources through the overall school budget;
2. set priorities in funding provision and curriculum development over a three-year period;
3. gain support (among governors, non-arts staff, and parents) by showing that arts provision and development are grounded in financial acumen and control;
4. compile an arts development plan linked to the school development plan;
5. devise an effective scheme to evaluate arts provision;
6. organise 'blue skies' sessions within a realistic financial environment.

The Audit Commission, which carries out 'value-for-money' studies of public bodies, concludes that there is no blueprint or magic formula for what works or by which to make decisions on resources (see *Money Matters: School funding and resource management*, Audit Commission, November 2000). Effective resource management relies on the quality of judgement exercised by staff and governors about where best to target resources.

Setting priorities

The first step in setting priorities is to answer two key questions:

1. What do we want to do?
2. What resources do we have in order to do what we want to do?

The answers can give plans both reality and sustainability.

Priorities for the arts have to be set within a number of different but related contexts. These include national targets for raising standards, the LEA's education development plan, the local authority's cultural strategy, the school development plan, the conclusions of the latest Ofsted inspection, the expertise of staff, the interests and needs of the pupils, and the quality of local and regional arts resources available beyond the school. There should also be a consideration of relevant educational research and of development in the arts themselves.

Key questions to ask here include:

1. Do we want to balance sustaining and developing existing art forms in the school with introducing new art forms?
2. What new art forms do we want to introduce, and why?
3. What additional or re-allocated resources do we need in order to:
   - maintain arts provision at its current level,
   - raise standards and quality in one of more arts subject,
   - develop new areas of arts provision?
4. What additional administrative support do the arts staff need in order to:
   - maintain arts provision at its current level,
   - raise standards and quality in one or more arts subject,
   - develop new areas of arts provision?

Once you have considered these questions, make a list of priorities for the financial and other resources you need, and set them against actual and potential sources for these purposes.

In addition, agree clear targets for what any new spending or resource allocation is expected to achieve, using those targets to assess what is achieved in the future.

Being effective

Keeping control of the arts budget and ensuring it is used to best effect requires close contact with, and support for, members of the arts team. This can encourage not just overall financial responsibility but also a readiness to look for and suggest better ways of using resources across the whole team. For example:

Information

- give all arts staff details of the arts budget and their spending allocation;
- ensure everyone knows about the options open to, and decisions made about, spending on the arts.

Monitoring

- agree benchmark targets and monitor how effectively the budget is being spent and resources used;
- establish where there is room for improvement.

Support

- offer staff with help on financial matters;
- ensure training and advice on managing finance and resources that are available to staff who want it;
- collaborate on making improvements in the use of resources.

Funding arts partnerships

An arts partnership can be as modest as buying in an artist for a day to a major project with a national arts organisation (see also section on *Partnerships and evaluation*, pages 156–63). Whatever the size of, and context for, the partnership, you need to budget for it. The funding can come from the school budget, the partner-organisation, fundraising by the school or the parent-teacher or home-school association, Lottery awards, outside sponsors or grant-giving agencies, or a combination from two or more of these sources.

The QCA and ACE have issued joint guidance to schools on developing arts partnerships (see *From Policy to Partnership: Developing the arts in schools*, QCA/ACE, March 2000). This lists eight items that should be taken into account when planning a 'partnership budget':

1. fees for artists and arts organisations, including the time needed to plan, prepare for, and evaluate the partnership;
2. fees for any commissioned work;
3. artists' travel and subsistence;

4. supply cover to enable teachers to plan, be involved in, and evaluate the partnership;

5. materials and equipment;

6. transport costs and tickets to attend arts venues;

7. costs of presenting final work;

8. insurance.

Funding through the school

A wide range of funding sources are currently available for arts activities. The main source of funding is the school budget, backed up by any fundraising through the PTA, school events, and so on.

The **Standards Fund** is the Government's main channel for targeting funds towards the national priorities which LEAs and schools are expected to act on. It includes dedicated funding for LEA music services. But the arts as a whole can become a crucial element in many of the priorities, even though they are not specifically identified in the Fund's categories.

Look at the six funding categories in the DfES guidance (currently *Standards Fund 2002–2003*, LEA/054/2001, September 2000) and consider how they might legitimately support activities, programmes and initiatives involving the arts:

1. **school improvement:** enabling schools to raise levels of achievement, including meeting the targets set out in their school development plan;

2. **inclusion:** removing barriers to progress, addressing special educational needs, and promoting social inclusion;

3. **standards and curriculum:** raising standards across the curriculum, which includes maintaining and extending the broadest possible access to music services;

4. **diversity and excellence:** raising performance achieving excellence and transforming school education through a targeted programme of support, mainly around the Excellence in Cities programme and specialist and beacon schools;

5. **teachers and support:** developing the skills and enhancing the status of all teachers and headteachers, supporting the modernisation of the teaching profession, and further developing the role of teaching assistants;

6. **capital and infrastructure:** raising educational standards through effective investment in school buildings and infrastructure, including the capacity to use information and communications technology (ICT).

National Lottery-backed funding programmes

The **regional arts lottery programme (RALP)** offers project and capital funding for community schemes. Schools are eligible to apply for arts partnerships projects which also provide clear benefits to the wider community. (Contact your regional arts board.)

Awards for All helps local groups, which include schools, and is based on very specific funding criteria. (Contact the scheme on 0845 600 2040.)

New Opportunities Fund (NOF) is awarding a total of £205 million across the UK for projects in half of all secondary and special schools and a quarter of all primary schools by 2001. The scheme gives priority to projects addressing the needs of the most disadvantaged pupils. Arts activities are an important element in such projects. (Contact NOF on 0845 00 00 121; website: www.nof.org.uk.)

Study support

NOF has allocated £200 million to expand study support out of school hours. **Study support** embraces homework clubs, study centres, mentoring, and creative and physical activities. Activities must be of high quality, wide-ranging, and relevant to pupils' needs and interests.

Education Extra, the foundation for after school activities, plays a key role in developing study support. It publishes guides and codes of practice, organising and evaluating projects, and runs a grants scheme for innovation and excellence. (Contact Education Extra at 17 Old Ford Road, London E2 9Pl; phone 020 8709 9900, website: www.education extra.org.uk.)

Arts sector initiatives

New Generation Audiences (NGA) Project was launched in 2000 to:

1. introduce young people to cultural events many would not normally attend;
2. encourage their ongoing involvement in such pursuits; and
3. develop their creativity, research and ICT skills through building virtual learning communities to discuss the events they attend.

Schools, teachers and young people can go online to share knowledge, discuss performances, and prepare for visits via relevant websites. Venues can keep in contact with pupils through their school career and beyond through e-mail, and offer discounted or free tickets for events. By January 2001, 36 arts venues and organisations were part of the scheme. (Contact NGA through the Learning Circuit on 020 8392 3785, or www.learning-circuit.co.uk.)

New Audiences Fund, set up by DCMS in 1998, awards annual grants to support young people and those with few opportunities to attend the arts, such as those living in isolated rural areas or deprived inner city areas. The programme is managed by ACE and the ten regional arts boards. Some projects are based in or involve schools during or out-of school hours. (Contact your regional arts board.)

National Foundation for Youth Music offers music opportunities for children and young people up to the age of eighteen. Its four programmes (Dynamo, First Steps, Music Maker, and Singing Challenge) offer schools and other organisations, plus individual pupils and teachers a range of projects for teaching, learning and making music. It is also developing a series of Music Action Zones in different parts of the country in order to bring communities together, share good practice, and develop young people's skills. (Contact Youth Music on 020 7902 1060, or www.youthmusic. org.uk. It is based at One America Street, London SE1 ONE phone 020 7902 1060; fax 020 7902 1061; e-mail nfym@youth-music.org.uk.)

▰ Trusts and foundations

Numerous private trusts and foundations run grant schemes to support the development and provision of arts education for children and young people. We have listed those in Appendix 2. Seeking funding from such organisations is time-consuming, ideally requires some knowledge of the specific trust or foundation, and demands specific skills in appropriate bidding. However arts activities, especially those going beyond the core classroom timetables, do attract grants.

▰ 5.2 Accommodation and facilities

Some aspects of the design of school premises are generally rather well considered, for instance gymnasia, libraries, science laboratories. However, others are not, for instance reception offices, pastoral middle-managers' rooms, and much of the specific accommodation for arts (perhaps the worst is for dance).

Consider also the need for a performing venue. There are no figures for how many schools have an adequate hall with suitable platform, full blackout, facilities for stage lighting, suitable entrances for audiences, and privacy. Very few have well designed audience layout, only a fraction having tiered seating. In the years after World War II most new schools were built with halls that were not all-purpose, had good stages, and were suitable for assemblies, drama lessons, and music and drama performances. In the 1960s economies came in, and many were also built as through-ways for movement round the school, difficult to convert for focused, stage performances. Those schools with purpose-designed theatres had a substantial advantage.

At the start of this century the DfEE combined with the Department for Culture, Media and Sport, the Arts Council of England, and Sport England to produce a very thoughtful and encouraging booklet of advice. *Designing Space for Sports and Arts* encourages primary schools to work with others to provide arts and sports facilities for dual school and community use (DfEE, 2000). It shows how a performing space with good facilities can be combined with other uses.

Whilst it is extremely difficult to raise the funding for expensive extensions and adaptations, it is sometimes possible to gain funding from specific central government grants, national lottery, Education Action Zone funding, major charitable funds, and local businesses. Sometimes modest, ingenious adaptations allow major changes to the effectiveness of accommodation. Further, a school that has knowledgeably developed its vision of the optimum requirement is far better placed to obtain the funding than one that was not so planned. We shall highlight those aspects of accommodation and facilities that may benefit from additions.

■ Art

'Art' courses, as our book explores in Chapters 2 and 3, vary in the range of specialisms included, so that drawing and painting are often joined by print-making and photography, and sometimes by ceramics, sculpture, and the study of advertisements and other aspects of the media, including film-making. ICT will certainly play a part. The overlap with other arts is one of our main themes, and this is especially so with Design and Technology. Thus teaching, display, and storage space need to be related to the curriculum division of the courses. The library, ICT specialist rooms, and display spaces in cabinets elsewhere in the school also need designing as an aspect of the art teaching.

Of course, as with the other specialist art courses, the number of teaching spaces will relate to the number of classes likely to be timetabled simultaneously – with Key Stage 4 and post-sixteen options this is not easy to calculate. If possible, it is good to complement the full-class teaching spaces with smaller, untimetabled ones for special sub-group activities. Indeed, an art suite benefits, for instance, from a seminar space for viewing film or slides separately from the practical area. Similarly a dark room for screen-printing and development, and also for posing for photographs, is also valuable.

Size is very important: the range of specialised activities commonly included is increasing, and three-dimensional work, for instance, requires more space. Many schools have to work with teaching spaces that are somewhat too small, not because of insufficient single work spaces for pupils, but because of insufficient flexibility. The Architects and Building branch of the DfEE recommended just before the turn of the century a minimum ratio for a class of 30: for two-dimensional work as between 79 and 105m^2, rising to between 103 and 115m^2 'where there is a bias towards working in three dimensions or doing screen printing on textiles' (p.4).

The DfEE *Building Bulletin 89* (1998) sets out the details of equipment and layout admirably fully for a variety of patterns of use. Storage is particularly important. We also recommend the concept of a 'staff/resource area', 'where pupils can go in small groups and study away from the messier environment of the classroom' (DfEE, 2000, p.20).

Dance

The least wellhoused of the arts in schools nationally has long been dance. In 1983 Her Majesty's Inspectors of Schools in a review of dance in schools gave devastating figures and descriptions: of the 35 schools visited 'only seven schools had a space designated as a dance studio; three had been purpose built but the others, converted from former classroom or canteen spaces, provided an inappropriate dance environment' (HMI, 1983, p.5). HMI confirmed most people's impressions: 'Money was rarely allocated specifically for dance; sound equipment was usually inadequate and fewer than a third of the schools had access to VTR' (HMI, 1983, p.5). We do not have such precise figures for the early years of the twenty-first century. However, although a number of schools have installed excellent dance-teaching studios in recent years, the overall provision is still weak, with few purpose-designed spaces and many occasions of part-time use of multipurpose halls, of which the worst are often those used for pupil lunches. Gymnasia, though often used, are rarely suitable aesthetically, atmospherically, acoustically, or by association. Some drama studios are excellent, though a number are too small. If dual- or multi-use is essential, it is important to find ways of meeting the dance-specific needs and this can often be done with some ingenuity.

The dance teaching requirements include:

1. sufficient space
2. a good, level, stable, well-surfaced floor
3. privacy from passers by
4. an undistracting surround, with only high-level windows
5. reasonable quiet
6. good, smooth, overall light
7. adjacent changing facilities
8. good storage space, accessible but suitably protected by doors
9. excellent sound equipment.

We have seen multipurpose halls (especially when dining is not one of the functions) work well if the acoustics are suitable and the wall finishing and lighting given a theatrical and performing touch. It is successful only if there is physical or psychological isolation, and delicate attempts at sensitive movement are not seen by those having to use the hall as a throughway (an unfortunate 1960s central government economy recommendation to save building cost for corridors). For performances, use of a good-size stage with an auditorium is essential.

Drama

Drama-teaching rooms are very similar to those required for dance, requiring space, privacy, good acoustics, and even 'stage' lighting for the shaping of the teaching space. Rostrum blocks are used considerably more often, and thus this additional storage space is required. If the overall numbers of spaces is sufficient for the number of pupils and the timetabling, studios could successfully be used for both dance and drama. Of course, the halls for performing to an audience with full scenery and lighting are essential for drama as well as dance. The DfEE has stressed the educational and community value of such public spaces in its guidelines on space for sport and the arts (DfEE, 2000).

Music

In general the specific needs of music teaching have been better incorporated into traditional school design. Many boarding and day schools have music suites, even separate buildings, which combine large-group rehearsing spaces with a whole-class teaching room, individual practice and teaching rooms with recording control units and storage. However, very many schools have inadequate accommodation. The optimum requirements are more architecturally difficult than classrooms for most secondary courses (c.f. *Building Bulletin* on music, DfEE, 1997).

The first difficulty is the need for a number of inter-related rooms. Music classrooms are required in sufficient number to accommodate all the classes within the restrictions of the school timetable. Timetabling for music classes can have some awkward placements because of Key Stage 4 option blocks and Key Stage 3 rotations that make it impossible to have as high a proportion of room usage as English or Mathematics. These main teaching classrooms should be en suite with related smaller rooms, for instance: a larger classroom also usable as a 'recital room'; group-rehearsal rooms for small instrumental groups; small individual practice and tuition rooms; instrument store; and a recording/control room.

The recording of pupils' work is a very important aspect of every music curriculum, as is listening to the pupils' own recordings and a wide range of other recordings. Compared with most aspects of a school's work, Music requires more small-group or individual work and usually offers far more small-group and individual tuition outside timetabled classes. Thus the small rooms are essential. The main Music classrooms themselves will require space, facilities, and ambience for a range of activities, for instance:

1. whole-class composing and performing, including instrumental and singing

2. whole-class listening to music, having explanations by the teacher, seminars, discussions, evaluations

3. whole-class keyboard playing

4. research by small groups or individuals

5. composing individually or in small groups

6. performances by small groups or individuals to the whole class

7. various forms of written assessment of the whole class.

The space has to be acoustically appropriate for all the musical activities, without picking up interference from outside (for example traffic noises) or disturbing other rooms of quieter study. The shape should have good acoustics, for instance not being cuboid or having sound-focusing ceiling structures such as barrel vaulting. The necessary floor space for a class of 30 has been estimated by the DfEE as between 60 and 70 square metres (*Building Bulletin* on music, DfEE, 1997, p.5). Awkward plans such as an L-shape inhibit flexibility.

Furniture for music-teaching rooms is very important and can be especially difficult with modern electronic needs. Tables or workbenches should be as flexible as possible, reasonably lightweight for easy mobility, and preferably standard in the suite of music rooms to facilitate re-grouping when required. For that purpose and for standing together on occasions, the tops must have firm edging to avoid splintering. Some modern tables have 'wire' management facilities, and these can be very helpful, such as a tray at the back of a table. 'Daisy chaining', where each table is serviced by a socket outlet in an adjacent table can be helpful, for example especially in ICT rooms, but more flexible cabling may be better for the lower requirements of electronic musical instruments.

Flexible seating is necessary, and thus stackable, plastic chairs are necessary for most purposes, with adjustable chairs for seating at a computer and for keyboards and percussion. Storage is especially necessary in music suites, for instruments (including keyboards), music, headphones, percussion, and recording equipment.

Conclusion

The arts require well-designed, spacious, fully equipped, and appropriately located suites of rooms. Imagination and practicality have to come together, and the school's main concourses have to support the arts with good display opportunities and assembling venues that can include performing to pupil or visitor audiences.

5.3 Technicians and support staff

Overall the UK has underdeveloped the role of 'support staff' or, to use the US phrase, 'para-professionals'. Indeed the contribution to the curriculum and pastoral care of the pupils has been very little studied with only one HMI report (HMI, 1992) and one research study (Mortimore, P. and J., 1994). The very limited number of support staff (often unhelpfully called 'non-teaching staff') are often undervalued and sometimes hardly incorporated into the full life of the school, and they are often illogically distributed, usually as the result of historical chance.

If you are a scientist you have technicians; if you are a PE teacher, nobody counts those instructors in the sports centres into your staff ratios. You have a technician if you have ceramics in your department but not if you have stage lighting. Nobody has ever thought out the pattern of support staff and there has been no central government study since the first ever HMI booklet in 1994. The Bullock report *A Language for Life* in 1975 specifically recommended that every secondary English department should have twenty hours 'internal' assistance a week for every five forms of entry in an eleven to eighteen school, and pro rata (Committee of Enquiry, 1975, pp.231–2). Nothing came of that and it has not been followed by other studies. Even the deeply considered study of the arts *All Our Futures* does not mention administrative or technical support, although it does recommend a role which does not include specific teaching:

> Where possible, school governing bodies should designate links between the school and cultural organisations and have an overview of the school's policies and programmes for creative and cultural education.
>
> (NACCCE, 1999, p.177)

Yes, but that is not possible for a teacher who is in front of a class and requires administrative time and facilities.

In the last years of the twentieth century there was a hesitant new interest, though the country lacked both intellectual analytic planning concepts and terminology. At one point in the 1990s, central government used 'support staff' as a term synonymous with 'classroom teacher assistant'. Probably the only academic study was P. and J. Mortimore's (1994), which explored new uses of 'non-teaching' staff in schools, none of which related specifically to the arts.

A study in 1992 by the Secondary Heads Association was an important introduction to help schools 'review their support staff provision'. It was clear that few LEAs and schools had a rational philosophy and policy. Indeed, the survey found that: 'Many secretaries felt that they were treated as second-class citizens by teaching staff.' (Warrington, 1992, p.*i*) Despite the helpfulness of this short survey and coherent introduction, there was virtually no coverage of the arts – except IT technicians 'to be able to assist with the desktop publishing material'.

The new century has seen a fresh, though vaguely defined, concern for administration. More than one education minister has given a generally supportive statement for the need, for example Estelle Morris in 2001: 'a greater role for school bursars . . . more clerical and administrative support for heads and teachers'. Significantly, the ATL (Association of Teachers and Lecturers) and PAT (Professional Association of Teachers) now include some of those who work in a school without being teachers as affiliated members.

Sport England has led a major move forward by encouraging, devising, training, and establishing in their *Active Schools* project the role of those for whom they have coined a new technical term AOTTs: 'Adults Other Than Teachers'. There will be a support pack specifically for schools inducting AOTTs for the sports life of the school:

> *Adults Other Than Teachers (AOTTs) are coaches, sports development officers and volunteers who assist in delivering physical education and out-of-school-hours sports activities. All AOTTs should work under the supervision of a teacher and should never be left on their own with a group.*
>
> (Sport England, 2001)

The major study by PriceWaterhouse Coopers on *Teacher Workload Study* (2000) makes a recommendation for 'an enhanced role for support staff', but is weak on the arts. The content, materials, equipment and activity of the arts also require 'para-professional' support. This support at present is available only to the studio arts, where for instance, the techniques and technical aspects of oil paintings – the treatment of wood or canvas, the under layers, the use of colour, the sources of pigments, and perspective – are explained. Similarly, the 'staging' techniques and other aspects of the performing arts require additional support.

Some schools organise certificated 'Theatre Technology' courses for Key Stage 4 where the occupational world of theatres, broadcasting, newspapers, book publishing, and art galleries are explored. Skilled technicians not only help the teachers and improve the conditions, but they also give direct educational benefit by teaching skills and understanding if properly briefed and utilised. Technicians in Design and Technology and Science departments are well established and regarded as essential. Schools need technicians for music, (especially, but not only, ICT), drama, and dance, and the visual and three-dimensional arts.

Many of the obvious components of a whole-school arts curriculum policy have financial and administrative requirements beyond that of classroom/studio teaching and which are not, indeed, compatible with a class-teaching timetable, for example:

1. administering, booking, hanging, and publicising visual art exhibitions

2. editing, designing, and publishing editions of pupil writing

3. linking with the full range of local and national agencies (see next section)

4. booking in visiting musical, acting, and dance performers

5. putting together photographs of locally significant examples of architecture, for example for Key Stage 2 'local history' and Key Stage 3 visual awareness

6. Devising displays and performances linking national and international dates and events to the school's overall arts curriculum, e.g. the anniversary of a musician, dancer, writer.

Further, involving the local and national artistic world requires more research, planning, administration, and financial arrangements than most school courses. Publicity costs, admission charges, visiting performers' fees, insuring display material, and hire charges all must be taken into account.

A strong case needs to be made for specialist, knowledgeable, and creative administration for the support of the full arts programme. Financial problems will of course be there, but we believe attitudinal ones are just as serious, and many schools have now shown that the modest funding can be found if a school carefully considers its support-staff needs. Indeed, one of us long ago argued the cost-effectiveness of support staff: 'By under-investing in para-professionals, we have wasted part of the massive investment in teachers.' (Marland, 1978, p.1.)

5.4 Partnerships and evaluation

Most aspects of a school's work benefit from a range of relationships with the communities a school serves. This is especially true for the development of the arts in a school. Schools must build an equal partnership with other schools and with arts organisations and artists, rather than just accept what they are offered, or agree to a one-off activity with no preparation or follow-up. The equality lies not so much in offering the same, but exchanging the best of what each has in order to meet the other's needs. This might be in terms of expertise, facilities, good practice, staff, curriculum development, involvement in projects with artists or arts organisations, and establishing joint networks and websites. One approach is to set up an arts education forum bringing together schools, arts venues and organisations, artists, and local authority departments. This has been done for example, in Milton Keynes (see *What If It Rains?* by Roy and Maggie Nevitt, 2000).

Collaboration and partnership are central themes in the government's policies for arts development in and through schools, and in unlocking pupils' and teachers' creative potential. This means a more coherent structure for such collaboration is being developed, both regionally and locally; and numerous sources of advice and information exchange are being provided through print and online.

Schools' first port of call for developing the arts and cultural activities, is their local authority, which should be developing its own Local Cultural Strategy, and their regional arts board. Both would also be direct or indirect sources of funding and other resources, for activities and projects.

In the future, there are two main 'structures' most likely to benefit schools. First, new Creative Partnerships are being developed across the country. These partnerships will be established between schools; professional cultural organisations – performing companies and ensembles, arts venues, media and other creative industries, higher education institutions, and so on; and individual artists across the arts and creative industries. The aims are to complement and enhance the work of teachers; inject additional cultural resources and activities into schools; establish a network of cultural or artistic mentors for pupils and teachers; and ensure every pupil can benefit from such Partnerships, especially those embarking on the new Pupil Learning Credits.

Second, the government is pressing ahead with enlarging the proportion of specialist schools and ensuring that there is much more collaboration and sharing between these schools and other local schools. Where such collaboration currently exists, the benefits have been clear for all categories of school involved. Linked to this is the new Artsmark scheme which, as it expands, will also open up more opportunities for partnerships between schools.

The current re-organisation of the state sector of schooling is bringing a new complexity to the way schools are organised and in what they do. To some this is seen as a threat to the smooth running of a school, and as a process that hinders rather than helps because of the additional pressures of coping with change. But the very diversity that should ensue from these changes also offers an exciting challenge to schools.

Schools have the opportunity to enhance or rebuild their cultural or arts strategies and provision by making the kind of new partnerships mentioned above. In doing so, they can point to the government's white paper *Schools: Achieving success* (DfES, September 2001), which embraces the arts and their importance in children's education more than any other education statement by a government (outside an official report). Read alongside the green paper issued around the same time *Culture and Creativity: The next ten years* (DCMS, March 2001), it is clear that the government is expecting schools to enhance and increase their arts provision. In turn, schools can hold the government to its cultural or arts 'pledges' in these policy documents. That includes the essential requirement to re-route, and open up, time, funding and other resources for the arts and creativity.

None of this can be done in a vacuum. Schools want to be able to develop a coherent philosophy, a firm internal curriculum and administrative structure, and a series of practical pathways for delivering opportunities both within and beyond the school. Guidance on all these aspects is available from a range of sources. However, schools should look at them with a critical eye and seek to relate what they say to their specific needs and aspirations, the pupils, teachers, and local communities they work with, rather than follow the guidance slavishly. Always ask: is this the right direction for us? Extending boundaries and taking up new challenges is part of the process of providing effective and exciting creative opportunities.

Developing an arts policy which ensures entitlement to all pupils, embraces the wide range of art forms and new technologies, and is effective as a basis for developing arts partnerships, is the subject of the guide *From Policy to Partnership: Developing the arts in schools* (Qualifications and Curriculum Authority and Arts Council of England, March 2000). This should be consulted in conjunction with the guidance on carrying out an Arts Audit (see Chapter 3, Section 1).

However, there is another stage to the overall task of devising philosophy and provision for the arts which embraces both, and which can help to clarify a school's thinking not just on what is possible, but on what is desirable. It is evaluation, or what can more appropriately be seen as 'developing a culture of reflection'.

There are two key sources for this activity, which have somewhat different, but largely complementary, approaches. The Arts Council of England (ACE) and the ten Regional Arts Boards (RABs) have issued a guide to evaluating arts education projects *Partnerships for Learning* (Felicity Woolf, ACE, October 1999), which forms one of the basic guidance documents for the Artsmark scheme.

The guide sees evaluation in terms of: making judgements based on evidence about the value and quality of the project; being an open and clear process which involves all the partners in the project, including the participants; and helping with decision making during the project, and for future projects.

The main purposes of evaluation are: to improve practice during the project and subsequent projects and to show what happened as a result of the project.

Essentially, the aim is to show that arts projects are a good way to learn, offer various benefits, and, more pragmatically, are well run and a valuable use of scarce resources.

Evaluation starts before the project. In an initial planning stage, the project partners must agree why they are doing the project, what they want to achieve, and how success will be identified. This sets the parameters for what and how to evaluate, in order to move on to the second stage of collecting the evidence required. This evidence can then be brought together, analysed and interpreted. There is then a period of reflecting on what has been learnt from the evaluation and how to use those lessons to develop and refine subsequent projects. The final stage is reporting on and sharing the outcomes and evidence of the project. This gives us five stages: planning; collecting evidence; assembling and interpreting; reflecting and moving forward and reporting and sharing.

A checklist for each stage offers a series of questions which schools can address:

Stage 1: planning

1. Who will have overall responsibility for evaluation?
2. How much will evaluation cost in time and money?
3. Have review sessions during and after the project been timetabled?
4. What are the project's aims, objectives and measures of success?
5. Are they acceptable to all partners, including those taking part?
6. Are they realistic?
7. Do they take into account what might be achieved in the short and long term?
8. How will unexpected outcomes be recognised and valued?

Stage 2: collecting evidence

1. Will evidence be collected before, during and/or at the end of the project?
2. How will the project be documented?
3. Will the evidence collected reveal what all the partners need to know?
4. Are the methods of collecting evidence flexible enough to reveal unexpected outcomes?
5. Will the evidence be convincing and show a range of viewpoints?
6. How will people taking part be asked what they think of the project?
7. Do the methods for collecting evidence take account of equal opportunities issues?
8. Are the methods manageable?
9. Has the use of evidence been agreed?

Stage 3: assembling and interpreting

1. Has data been changed into information?
2. Has evidence been interpreted convincingly?
3. Has the information been organised in advance for presentation at evaluation meetings, during and at the end of the project?
4. Does the presentation show if aims and objectives have been achieved?
5. Have unexpected outcomes been included?
6. Has descriptive documentation been kept to a minimum?
7. Has the information been put together to give an overview of the project?

Stage 4: reflecting and moving forward

1. How will partners reflect on the evaluation?
2. What were the key findings from the evaluation?
3. How did the project compare with others?
4. What decisions and changes should now be made?

Stage 5: reporting and sharing

1. What methods of reporting are needed, which will satisfy all partners?
2. How have the findings of the evaluation been shared with people who took part?
3. Who else should be told about the project?
4. What do they need to know?
5. What would be the best way of recording the project and presenting the findings of the evaluation?

One of the most critical issues surrounding collaborative projects is the compatibility between the desired outcomes and the indicators of success of school and arts organisation. In short, how far are they using the same criteria for assessing the effectiveness and therefore the continuing development of partnerships for arts education?

The challenge is to find appropriate ways of supporting the arts in schools through programmes and projects that are sensitive to the needs of teachers and designed in close partnership with them. That is the conclusion of *Evaluating Education Programmes in Arts Organisations*, a study carried out by Exeter University professor Malcolm Ross funded by the Calouste Gulbenkian Foundation. This study focused on the ways that arts organisations were devising programmes for schools, how far they met schools' needs, and how a more effective process of putting together and evaluating such programmes could be developed. The key elements of partnerships between schools and arts organisations should be to ensure: quality, stability and continuity; intellectual rigour and practical coherence to provision and assessment; and close and sustained engagement with the emotional and aesthetic development of all pupils.

This requires considerable and considered negotiation between school and arts organisation, and more specifically between teacher and artist. The key question to be addressed and resolved has to be: what is the rationale for our partnership? This will help to determine both the content, desired outcomes and evaluation of the project.

There is, of course, a third partner in any such project: the pupil. As far as practicable, their views must also be canvassed about a project's aims, content and evaluation. Otherwise the project risks being something that is done to pupils rather than with them. Malcolm Ross explains:

> *An evaluation which does not allow the individual student an opportunity confidentially to express an opinion of the character and quality of the educational encounter is virtually worthless in this field. Similarly, such an evaluation has to be seen as coming from the institution (or from an outside source) and not from the teacher/tutor concerned with the project. A procedure needs to be built that respects the local situation and which 'triangulates' (and thereby renders plausible and reliable) the complementary evaluations of the programme makers, the clients and disinterested experts.*
>
> (Ross, 2000, p.25)

Devising and evaluating collaborative projects must take account of the pupil's creative process. This, according to a model proposed by Rom Harre in *Personal Being* (Blackwell, 1983) embraces:

1. the pupil's tradition and the cultural stock (conventionalisation);
2. the pupil's personal taste, voice and style (appropriation);
3. the use of symbol and the making of symbols in the arts (transformation); and
4. the field of cultural transactions, including production and evaluation (publication).

To this is added a model of reflective practice in the teaching of the arts (see Donald Schon's *The Reflective Practitioner: How professionals think in action*, Avebury, 1983):

1. the practitioner's repertoire of **practical skills**;
2. the practitioner's system of **values**;
3. the over-arching **theory** informing the practitioner's practical strategies; and
4. the **roles** that the practitioner frames for him/herself and the pupils.

This, Ross proposes, leads us to a four-part evaluation matrix (essentially a list of key questions) which can fulfil the requirements discussed above, and encourage the culture of reflection. In effect, while coming from different perspectives on the philosophy and practice of arts education and the potential partnerships that can drive it forward, these two sources of guidance can be complementary. Taken together they can influence the thinking within and across the partners involved.

1. Practical skills

Key issue: What teaching skills are needed to cover the pupil's four areas of learning in the arts – and does the teacher have these skills?

Key questions:

1. What teaching skills are needed to introduce pupils to the repertoire and conventions of the arts?
2. How might a pupil best be encouraged to develop a personal voice and style?
3. How do we teach pupils to make, use and handle artistic symbols?
4. How do we teach pupils to engage in the transactions of the arts, including the practice of presentation and criticism, and making use of artistic institutions?

2. Values

Key issue: What values might inform the teacher's judgement in respect of pupils' work – and how might these judgements be expressed?

Key questions:

5. What values should determine choices of curriculum content? How do we appraise conventional learning?
6. How do we value and evaluate a pupil's artistic style and preferences?

7. What criteria should determine our professional response to the images produced by pupils and to their feelings about the images of other artists?

8. How do we judge the quality of a pupil's engagement with artistic institutions?

3. Theory

Key issue: What pedagogy informs our teaching – and what belief system of teaching and learning about the arts operates within our arts teaching practice?

Key questions:

9. How do pupils best learn about the heritage and acquire practical know-how in the arts?

10. What is style, and how do pupils appropriate artistic conventions?

11. What is creativity in the arts, and how does it develop?

12. What work do the arts do in the world, and how do pupils become participants in the public transactions and discourses of the arts?

4. Roles

Key issue: What pedagogic relationships are most appropriate for each aspect of learning in the arts: instruction, demonstration, dialogue, partnering, conversing, bearing witness?

Key questions:

13. What roles are most effective for teaching tradition and practical know-how in the arts?

14. How should one be a teacher in relation to a pupil's style?

15. How should a teacher be involved in the pupil's expressive act?

16. How can teachers reconcile unconditional commendation with objectivity and detachment?

How the questions fit together

		Schon model		
Harre model	skills	values	theory	roles
convention	1	5	9	13
appropriation	2	6	10	14
transformation	3	7	11	15
publication	4	8	12	16

APPENDIX 1: ARTS AND CURRICULUM ORGANISATIONS

Arts Council of England (ACE), 14 Great Peter Street, London SW1P 3NQ; tel. 020 3330100; www.artscouncil.org.uk. **Arts Council of Wales**, 9 Museum Place, Cardiff CF10 3NX; tel. 02920 376500. **Artsmark**, c/o ACE, 14 Great Peter Street, London SW1P 3NQ; freephone 0800 560196; www.artsmark.org.uk. **Artworks**: the National Children's Art Awards, PO Box 105, Rochester, Kent, ME2 4BE; tel. 0870 2412762; www.art-works.org.uk. **Crafts Council**, 44a Pentonville Road, London N1 4AA; tel. 020 7806 2500; www.craftscouncil.org.uk. **Department for Culture, Media and Sport (DCMS)**, 2–4 Cockspur Street, London, SW1Y 5DH; tel. 020 7211 6000; www.culture.gov.uk. **Department for Education and Skills (DfES)**, Sanctuary Buildings, Great Smith Street, London SW1P 3BT; tel. 0870 0012345; www.dfes.gov.uk. **Demos**, The Mezzanine, Elizabeth House, 39 York Road, London SE1 7NQ, tel. 020 7401 5330; www.demos.co.uk. **Design Council**, 34 Bow Street, London WC2E 7DL; tel. 020 7420 5200; i@designcouncil.org.uk; www.designcouncil.org.uk. **Drawing Power**: the campaign for drawing, 7 Gentleman's Row, Enfield EN2 6PT; tel. 020 8351 1719; www.drawingpower.org.uk. **Education Extra**, 17 Old Ford Road, London E2 9PL; tel. 020 8709 9933; www.educationextra.org.uk. **Engage**: the national association for gallery education, 1 Herbal Hill, Clerkenwell, London EC1R 5EJ; tel. 020 7278 8382; info@engage.org. **Estyn**: HM Inspectorate for Education and Training in Wales, Phase 1, Government Buildings, Ty Glas Road, Llanishen, Cardiff CF14 5FQ; tel. 02920 325000. **Federation of Music Services (FMS)**, 6 Berwick Courtyard, Berwick St Leonard, Salisbury, Wiltshire SP3 5SN; tel. 01747 820042; www.fp.federationmusic.f9.co.uk. **National Assembly for Wales** (Education Department, NAED), Fourth Floor, Crown Buildings, Cathays Park, Cardiff CF10 3NQ; tel. 02920 825111. **National Association for the Teaching of English (NATE)**, 50 Broadfield Road, Sheffield S8 0XJ; tel. 0114 255 5419. **National Dance Teachers Association**, 47 Grove Hill Road, Camberwell, London SE5 8DF; tel. 020 727 4052; **National Foundation for Educational Research (NFER)**, The Mere, Upton Park, Slough, Berkshire

SL1 2DQ; tel. 01753 574123; www.nfer.ac.uk. **National Foundation for Youth Music**, One America Street, London SE1 0NE; tel. 020 7902 1060; www.youthmusic.org.uk. **National Resource Centre for Dance**, University of Surrey, Guildford GU2 5XH; tel. 01483 259316. **National Society for Education in Art and Design (NSEAD)**, The Gatehouse, Corsham Court, Wiltshire SN13 0BZ; tel. 01249 714825; www.nsead.org. **Office for Standards in Education (OFSTED)**, Alexandra House, 29-33 Kingsway, London WC2B 6SE; tel. 020 7421 6800; www.ofsted.gov.uk. **Poetry Book Society**, 45 East Hill, London SW18 2QZ, tel. 020 8870 8403; **Poetry Society**, 22 Betterton Street, London WC2H 9BU, tel. 020 7420 9880; **Qualifications and Curriculum Authority (QCA)**, 29 Bolton Street, London W1Y 7PD; tel. 020 7905 5555; www.qca.org.uk. **Royal Institute of British Architects (RIBA)**, 66 Portland Place, London W1B 1AD; tel. 020 7580 5533; www.architecture.com. **Royal Society for the encouragement of Arts, manufactures and commerce (RSA)**, 8 John Adam Street, London WC2N 6EZ; tel. 020 7930 5115; www.rsa.org.uk. **Sainsbury's Pictures for Schools, Arts Sponsorship Department**, J Sainsbury plc, Stamford House, Stamford Street, London SE1 9LL; tel. 020 795 8181. **Sciart: Partnerships in Science and Art**, The Wellcome Trust, 210 Euston Road, London NW1 2BE; tel. 020 7611 8538; www.wellcome.ac.uk/sciart. **The Tagore Centre UK**, Alexandra Park Library, Alexandra Park Road, London N22 4UJ; tel. 020 8368 4302.

APPENDIX 2: TRUSTS AND FOUNDATIONS FOR ARTS FUNDING SUPPORT

Calouste Gulbenkian Foundation, 98 Portland Place, London W1N 4ET; tel. 020 7636 5313; info@gulbenkian.org.uk. **Clore Duffield Foundation**, Studio 3, Chelsea Manor Studios, Flood Street, London SW3 5SR; tel. 020 7351 6061; cloreduffield@aol.com. **Esmee Fairbairn Foundation**, 10/11 Park Place, London SW1A 1LP; tel. 020 7297 4700; www.esmeefairbairn.org.uk. **Paul Hamlyn Foundation**, 18 Queen Anne's Gate, London SW1H 9AA; tel. 020 7222 0601; www.phf.org.uk.

REFERENCES

Arts Council of England and MORI (2000) *Public Attitudes to the Arts*, ACE
Arts Council of England (1996) *Leading through Learning: consultative green paper on education and training*, ACE
Artworks (2001) *£2.68: survey of art and design resources in primary and secondary schools*, Clore Duffield Foundation
Assessment of Performance Unit (1985) *Discussion Document on the Assessment of Aesthetic Development Through Engagement in the Creative and Performing Arts*, APU
Audit Commission (2000) *Money Matters: school funding and resource management*, Audit Commission
Azzam, Khaled and Critchlow, Keith (1997) *The Arch in Islamic Architecture*, The Visual Islamic and Traditional Arts Department, The Prince of Wales's Institute of Architecture
Barton, Geoff (ed.) (1996) *Stories from Europe*, Longman Imprint Books
Bhinda, Madhu (ed.) (1996) *Stories from Africa*, Longman Imprint Books
Bhinda, Madhu (ed.) (1992) *Stories from Asia*, Longman Imprint Books
Blackstone, Tessa (1997) 'Heritage versus a creative recovery', *The Times*, 28 February
Bloom, H. (2000) *How to Read and Why*, Fourth Estate
Bloom, H. (1995) *The Western Canon*, Macmillan
Blunkett, David (2000) *Raising Aspirations in the 21st Century*, DfEE
Board of Education (1937) *Handbook of Suggestions for the Consideration of Teachers and Others Concerned with the Work of Elementary Public Schools*, HMSO
Bravmann, René A. (1983) *African Islam*, Smithsonian Institution Press, USA, and Ethnographica, London
Briggs, Asa (2001) *Michael Young, Social Entrepreneur*, Palgrave
Britten, Benjamin (1964) *On Receiving the First Aspen Award*, Faber and Faber
Bronowski, Jacob (1964) *Science and Human Values*, Penguin
Calouste Gulbenkian Foundation (1982) *The Arts in Schools: principles, practice and provision*, Calouste Gulbenkian Foundation, London
Calouste Gulbenkian Foundation (1980) *Dance Education and Training in Britain*, Calouste Gulbenkian Foundation, London
Central Advisory Council for Education (England) (1967) *Children and their Primary Schools*, ('The Plowden Report'), HMSO
Central Advisory Council for Education (England) (1963) *Half our Future*, ('The Newsom Report'), HMSO
Central Advisory Council for Education (England) (1959) *Fifteen to Eighteen* ('The Crowther Report') HMSO
Collins, A.F. (1938) *Book Crafts for Senior Pupils*, The Dryad Press
Committee of Enquiry (1975) *A Language for Life*, ('The Bullock Report'), HMSO
Consultative Committee of the Board of Education (1926) *The Education of the Adolescent*, ('The Haddow Report'), HMSO
Cook, Nicholas (1998) *Music: a very short introduction*, Oxford University Press
Copland, Aaron (1952) *Music and Imagination*, Harvard University Press
Crick, Francis (1989) *What Mad Pursuit?*, Weidenfeld and Nicholson
Cumming, Elizabeth and Kaplan, Wendy (1991) *The Arts and Crafts Movement*, Thames and Hudson
Davies, Hunter (1976) *The Creighton Report*, Hamish Hamilton

References

Department for Culture, Media and Sport (2001) *Culture and Creativity: The Next Ten Years*, DCMS
Department for Culture, Media and Sport (1999) *Arts and Sport: a report to the Social Exclusion Unit*, DCMS Policy Action Team 10, DCMS
Department for Education and Employment and Qualifications and Curriculum Authority (1999) *The National Curriculum, Handbook for secondary teachers in England*, and *Handbook for primary teachers in England*, DfEE & QCA
Department for Education and Employment (2000) *Designing Space For Sports And Arts*, DfEE
Department for Education and Employment (1998) *Art Accommodation in Secondary Schools, Building Bulletin 89*, The Stationery Office
Department for Education and Employment (1998) *School Prospectuses in Secondary Schools*, Circular 8/98, DfEE
Department for Education and Employment (1998) *School Prospectuses in Primary Schools*, Circular 7/98, DfEE
Department for Education and Employment (1997) *Music Accommodation in Secondary Schools, Building Bulletin 86*, The Stationery Office
Department for Education and Employment (1996) *Design and Technology Accommodation in Secondary Schools, Building Bulletin 81*, The Stationery Office
Department for Education and Skills (2001) *Schools: Achieving Success*, DfES
Department for Education and Skills (2001) *Standards Fund 2002–2003*, DfES guidance LEA/054/2001, DfES
Department of Education and Science (1977) *Curriculum 11–16, Working Papers by HMI Inspectorate: A contribution to current debate*, HMSO
DfEE and Qualifications and Curriculum Authority (1999) *The National Curriculum for England: Art and Design, English, Music, Physical Education*, DfEE and QCA
Donovan, Chris, Hicks, Alun and Naidoo, Beverley (1997) *Global Tales*, Longman
Dudley LEA Advisory Service & the Association of Advisors and Inspectors for Art and Design (AAIAD) (1996) *Art: a review of inspection findings 1995/96*, Ofsted
Dunkley, Ralph and Maddams, Joyce (1986) *Looking at the Built Environment*, Geography Teachers' Centre, City of London Polytechnic
Education Act 1996, HMSO
Education Reform Act 1988, HMSO
Eggleston, John (1971) 'Craft', in Whitfield, Richard (ed.) *Disciplines of the Curriculum*, McGraw-Hill
Elder, J.D. (1969) *From Congo Drum to Steelband*, University of the West Indies, Trinidad
Erikson, E.H. (1971) *Identity, Youth and Crisis*, Faber
Gill, Eric (1940) *Autobiography*, Jonathan Cape
Gray, Donald (2000) *Percy Dearmer, a Parson's Pilgrimage*, Canterbury Press
Hargreaves, David (1983) 'The Teaching of Art and the Art of Teaching: Towards an alternative view of aesthetic learning', in Hammersley, Martyn and Hargreaves, Andy, *Curriculum Practice: Some sociological case studies*, The Falmer Press
Harland, John, et al (2000) *Arts Education in Secondary Schools: effects and effectiveness*, National Foundation for Educational Research (NFER)
Harland, John and Kinder, Kay (eds.) (1999) *Crossing the Line: Extending young people's access to cultural venues*, Calouste Gulbenkian Foundation, London
Harre, Rom (1983) *Personal Being*, Blackwell
Hertrich, John (1998) 'Drama', in Ofsted, *The Arts Inspected*, Heinemann
Hillenbrand, Robert (1999) *Islamic Art and Architecture*, Thames and Hudson
Hipkin, John (1968) *The Peterloo Massacre*, Heinemann
HMI (1992) *Non-Teaching Staff in Schools: a review by HMI*, HMSO
HMI (1983) *Dance in Secondary Schools, a discussion paper*, DES
HMI (1979) *Aspects of Secondary Education in England, a survey by Her Majesty's Inspectors of Schools*, HMSO
Hodge, Alison (1982) *Nigeria's Traditional Crafts*, Ethnographica, London
Jones, Peter (1998) 'Art' in Ofsted, *The Arts Inspected*, Heinemann
Klein, Naomi (2000) *No Logo*, Flamingo

Kotewall, Robert and Smith, Norman L. (1968) *The Penguin Book of Chinese Verse*, Penguin
Lees, Jane and Plant, Sue (2000) *Passport, A Framework for Personal and Social Development*, Calouste Gulbenkian Foundation, London
Livingston, A. and I. (1992) *The Encyclopaedia of Graphic Design and Designers*, Thames and Hudson
London County Council (1947) *London School Plan*, LCC
Lorenz (1989) *Traditional Zambian Pottery*, Ethnographica, London
Mander, John (1948) *Old Bottles and New Wine, A Talk about Secondary Modern Schools*, Newnes Educational Publishing Company
Marland, Michael (1996) *Scenes from Plays*, Longman Imprint Books
Marland, Michael (1978) *The Teacher, the Ancillary, and Inner-City Education*, paper for the ILEA
Marland, Michael (1974) *The Question of Advertising*, Chatto & Windus Educational
Marland, Michael (1969) *Peter Grimes*, play adapted from Crabbe's poem, Heinemann
Marland, Michael (1969) *Towards the New Fifth*, Longman
Marland, Michael (1967) *Following the News, A Course in the Effective Reading of Newspapers*, Chatto & Windus
Marland, Michael and Rogers, Rick (1997) *The Art of the Tutor*, David Fulton
Marsh, Linda (1989) *Take a Look at You*, Longman Tutorial Resources, Book 2
Matarasso, F. (1997) *Use or Ornament? The social impact of participation in the arts*, Comedia
MacBeth, George (1984) *Poetry for Today*, Longman Study Texts
McAlhone, Beryl and Stuart, David (1996) *A Smile in the Mind*, Phaidon Press
McGuinness, Dr Carol (1999) *From Thinking Skills to Thinking Classrooms:* DfEE research report RR115, DfEE
McKinnon, Don (2000) speech to the Commonwealth Institute
McLeod, John (1991) *The Arts and the Year 2000*, National Arts in Australia Schools Project, Department of Education, Queensland, Australia
Medawar, Peter (1977) 'Intuition and Induction in Science', reprinted in *Pluto's Republic*, Oxford University Press
Micklethwait, Lucy (1996) *A Child's Book of Play in Art*, Dorling Kindersley
Miller, Peter, Chair of Working Party (1998) *Drama Sets You Free, a survey of drama in the curriculum of secondary schools*, Secondary Heads Association
Ministry of Education (1945) *The Nation's Schools, Their Plan and Purpose*, Ministry of Education Pamphlet No1, HMSO
Montford, Selma (1993) *Investigating Shopping*, Young Library
Morrell, Francis (1983) speech to the Inner London Education Authority
Morris, E.M. (2001) *Speech to the National Association of Headteachers*, 1 May
Mortimore, P. and J. (1994) *Managing Associate Staff, Innovation in Primary and Secondary Schools*, Paul Chapman
Moughtin, J.C. (1985) *Hausa Architecture*, Ethnographica, London
National Advisory Committee on Creative and Cultural Education (1999) *All Our Futures: Creativity, Culture and Education*, DfEE
Naylor, Gillian (1988) *William Morris by himself*, Little, Brown and Company
Nevitt, R. and M. (2001) *What If It Rains?*, Milton Keynes Arts Education Forum, Stantonbury Campus, Milton Keynes MK14 6BN www.mkaef.co.uk
Ofsted (1998) *The Arts Inspected*, Heinemann
PricewaterhouseCoopers (2001) *Teacher Workload Study*, PWC
Qualifications and Curriculum Authority and Arts Council of England (2000) *From Policy to Partnership: developing the arts in schools*, QCA/ACE
Qualifications and Curriculum Authority (2001) *Language at Work in Lessons, Literacy across the curriculum at Key Stage 3*, QCA Publications
Qualifications and Curriculum Authority (2000) *The National Curriculum for England: Citizenship at Key Stages 3 and 4*, QCA Publications
Redfern, H.B. (1986) *Questions in Aesthetic Education*, Allen & Unwin
Ree, Henry (1973) *Educator Extraordinary: The life and achievements of Henry Morris 1889–1961*, Longman
Richards, I.A. (1924) *Principles of Literary Criticism*, Routledge

References

Rogers, R. and Carter, K. (2001) *A Guide to Auditing the Arts in School*, RSA/ACE
Ross, Malcolm (2000) *Evaluating Education Programmes in Arts Organisations*, University of Exeter
Ross, Malcolm (1978) *The Creative Arts*, Heinemann Educational Books
Ross, Malcolm (1975) *Arts and the Adolescent*, Schools Council Working Paper 54, Evans/Methuen Educational
Royal Society of Arts (1998) *Investing in the Arts: how to carry out a school arts audit and compile an arts statement*, RSA
Savage, Jonathan and Challis, Mike (2001) *A Digital Arts Curriculum? Practical Ways Forward*, Debenham CEVC High School, Suffolk
Savage, Jonathan and Challis, Mike (2001) *Dunwich Revisited: Collaborative composition and performance with new technologies*, Debenham CEVC High School, Suffolk
Schon, Donald (1983) *The Reflective Practitioner: how professionals think in action*, Avebury
Seltzer, K. and Bentley, T. (1999) *The Creative Age: knowledge and skills for the new economy*, Demos
Sims, George R. (1968) *Prepare To Shed Them Now – the Ballads of George R. Sims Selected and introduced by Arthur Calder-Marshall*, Hutchinson
Smith, Rukshana (1989) *Sumitra's Story*, Bodley Head
SPAEM/OHMCI (1999) *Art, Drama and Music in Key Stages 3 and 4*, SPAEM/OHMCI
Sport England (2001) *Active Schools*, Sport England
Swanwick, Keith (1983) *The Arts in Education: Dreaming or Awake?* University of London Institute of Education
Tagore, Rabindranath (1996) *The Post Office*, translated by William Radice, Tagore Centre
Tagore, Rabindranath (1991) *Selected Short Stories*, translated by William Radice, Penguin
Tagore, Rabindranath (1988) *This World is Beautiful*, Tagore Centre
Tagore, Rabindranath (1985) *Selected Poems*, translated by William Radice, Penguin
Teacher Training Agency (1998) *Initial teacher training National Curriculum for Primary English*, Annex C to DfEE Circular, 4/98, TTA
Teacher Training Agency (1998) *Initial teacher training National Curriculum for Secondary English*, Annex F to DfEE Circular 4/98,TTA.
The Education (School Premises) Regulations 1991, Statutory Instrument No. 2 (1999) The Stationery Office
Tate, Nicholas (1996) *The Contribution of Design and Technology to the Curriculum*, School Curriculum and Assessment Authority and Design Council
Victoria and Albert Museum (1985) *Introduction to the Print Room*, V & A
Warrington, Michael (1992) *Managing Non Teaching Staff*, Secondary Heads Association
Watson, Derek (compiler) (1991) *Music Quotations*, Chambers
Whelan, Les M. (1991) *The Arts and Technology*, Department of Education, Queensland, Australia
Whitehead, Jack (1993) *Corners and Contrasts, An Architectural Walk in St James's*, RTZ Corporation
Wilkinson, Sue and Clive, Sue (2001) *Developing Cross-Curricular Learning in Museums and Galleries*, Trentham Books
Williams, D. Vincent and Allen, J. (2000) *Oklahoma*, sung by Billy Gilman on *One Voice*, recorded by Sony Music Entertainment Inc., USA, No: EK 62086
Williams, Geoffrey and Willson, Sandra (1999) *From Commonwealth to Common Wealth: The place of the arts in a multicultural society*, King George VI and Queen Elizabeth Foundation
Witkin, Robert (1974) *The Intelligence of Feeling*, Heinemann Education
Woolf, Felicity (1999) *Partnerships for Learning: a guide to evaluating arts education projects*, ACE and Eastern Arts Board
Young, Michael (Lord) (1988) speech to House of Lords 12 June, in *Hansard Official Reports*, HMSO
Zimelli, Umberto and Vergerio, Giovanni (1969) *Decorative Ironwork*, Hamlyn Publishing Group

INDEX

advertisements, analysis 38, 44–6
aesthetics, 38–9, 84–5
architecture
   intercultural links 24–5, 27–8
   materials 19, 28, 29–30
   National Curriculum place 26–7
   Schools 28, 29–30, 119–20
Art and Design 48, 149–50
artists 49, 107–9, 112–15
arts
   course contributions 83–5
   definitions 6, 19
   specific courses 81–3
Arts and Crafts Movement 24, 51–2, 56–7
assessment 69–70

book design 52–3, 56
budgeting *see* funding

ceramics 30–1, 32, 136
Citizenship 9, 111
community involvement 15, 79, 130–1
courses
   subject content 79–80
   subject specific 81–3, 132–3
Creative Partnerships 128–9, 131, 157
creativity
   definitions 8–9, 90
   process of 90–2
   thinking skills 91, 93–4
curriculum
   see also curriculum audits, National Curriculum
   delivery 18–81, 118–19, 132–3
   integration 17, 61, 94
   planning 78, 143–5
   subject planning 77, 82
   whole-school 3–4, 9–12, 18, 77–8
curriculum audits

aims and objectives 64–5
benefits 61–2
costs 66–7
headings 63–4, 68–71
management of 64–5, 66, 67
publicising 66, 71–2, 73
RSA guide 62
use of 72–3

dance
   facilities 138, 150–1
   gender bias 33
   integration 84
   National Curriculum requirements 15, 133
   performance 138
Demos, National Curriculum
   revisions 92
Design and Technology
   architecture 26–7
   integration 80–1, 82–3
   textiles 50
   wood/metalwork 58
drama
   facilities 150–1
   National Curriculum 33–4, 86, 133
   productions 136

English
   drama 33–4, 133
   integration 80
   literature 22–3, 39, 86
   media studies 42
evaluation 158–61, 162–3
exhibitions
   pupils' artworks 31, 119, 134
   visual arts 55, 124–6, 134–5, 136

funding
   assessing 68, 142
   control 144–5

external 145–6, 147–8
financial management 143
financial mapping 142–3
internal 146–7
sources 141, 145–6
surveys 139–40

graphic design 37–9, 87–8
Gulbenkian Report, Dance Education 1980 2–3, 33

integration
  arts contributions 80–1, 83–5
  National Curriculum subjects 14–15, 25–6, 79–80, 132–3
  whole curriculum 17, 61, 94
intercultural links 11–12, 20–2, 24–5, 34, 49, 51, 52, 57–8

literacy 40, 103–4, 105–6
literature
  National Curriculum 39
  world cultures 22–3
loan schemes, artworks, 54–5, 125
local education authorities (LEA) 69, 157

media studies 36–7
  analysis 43–6
  National Curriculum 41–2
metalwork 55–6, 57–8
Music
  facilities 151–3
  improvisation 76
  integration 84
  performance 74, 75–6
  recording 47, 137–8, 152

National Curriculum
  see also subjects by name
  architecture 26–7
  Demos revisions 92
  introduction of 13
  legal requirements 13–15, 132
  programmes of study 14–15
  subject integration 14–15, 25–6, 79–80, 132–3

Ofsted inspections 62, 66, 68

partnerships
  benefits 16
  equality in 156
  evaluation 158–63
  external 16, 47, 73, 102, 128–9, 157–8
  funding from 145–6

internal 16
other schools 70
policies 63
performances 74, 75, 136
Personal and Social Development (PSD)
  arts and 110, 115–17
  drama 36
  role play 115
  social inclusion 129–30
  tutorials 88–9
Personal, Social and Health Education (PSHE) 9, 11–12
Physical Education, dance 32–3, 133
policy statements 62–3, 72
primary schools
  architecture 29–30
  art appreciation 5–6
  arts funding 141–2
  ceramics 32
  dance 32–3
  drama 33–4, 35–6
  status of arts 8
  wood/metalwork 58–9
professional development 68, 92–3, 146
pupils
  artwork exhibitions 31, 119, 134
  involvement 69
  performances 136

regional arts lottery programme (RALP) 147
Religious Education (SACRE), arts integration 84, 86–7

resources
  architecture 19
  audits 63, 67
  loan schemes 54–5
  material forms 59
  schools as 28, 29–30
  sculpture 49
Ruskin, John 30

schools
  architecture 28, 29–30, 119–20
  communal life 118–19
  displays 31, 119
  performance facilities 148–9, 150–3
sculpture
  appreciation strategies 48–9
  Art and Design 48
  display 136
secondary schools
  architecture 28–9
  arts funding 140–1

secondary schools (*contd*)
  ceramics 31–2
  drama 34–5
  literature 40–1, 42
  status of arts 8
  tutorials 88–90
Standards Fund 146–7
subjects
  course contributions 79–80, 82, 132–3
  separation 14–15, 26, 77
support staff 153–4, 155–6

teachers
  arts audits 68
  initial training 41–2
  qualifications 63
  subject integration 94
television studies 37, 42–3
textiles 50, 51
typography 52–3, 56, 80

visual arts
  exhibitions 55, 124–6, 134–5, 136
  life skills 54
  loan schemes 54–5, 125
  observation 54
  pupils' 7, 31, 119

websites 4